AMATERASU

RETURN OF THE SUN

A
JAPANESE
MYTH

STORY BY
PAUL D. STORRIE

PENCILS AND INKS BY
RON RANDALL

OHOYASHIMA IS THE ANCIENT NAME FOR THE FIRST EIGHT ISLANDS OF **JAPAN**, CREATED BY THE GODS **IZANAGI** AND **IZANAMI**. THESE ISLANDS STILL BELONG TO THE MODERN COUNTRY OF **JAPAN**, BUT SOME OF THEIR NAMES HAVE CHANGED.

- **AWAJI** BELONGS TO THE MODERN **HYOGO** PREFECTURE (GOVERNMENT DISTRICT)

- **IKI** IS PART OF THE MODERN **NAGASAKI** PREFECTURE

- **IYO** WAS RENAMED **SHIKOKU**

- **OGI** IS PART OF THE MODERN **SHIMANE** PREFECTURE

- **SADO** IS PART OF THE MODERN **NIIGATA** PREFECTURE

- **TSUKUSHI** WAS RENAMED **KYUSHU**

- **TSUSHIMA** IS PART OF THE MODERN **NAGASAKI** PREFECTURE

- **YAMATO** WAS RENAMED **HONSHU**

AMATERASU
RETURN OF THE SUN

A JAPANESE MYTH

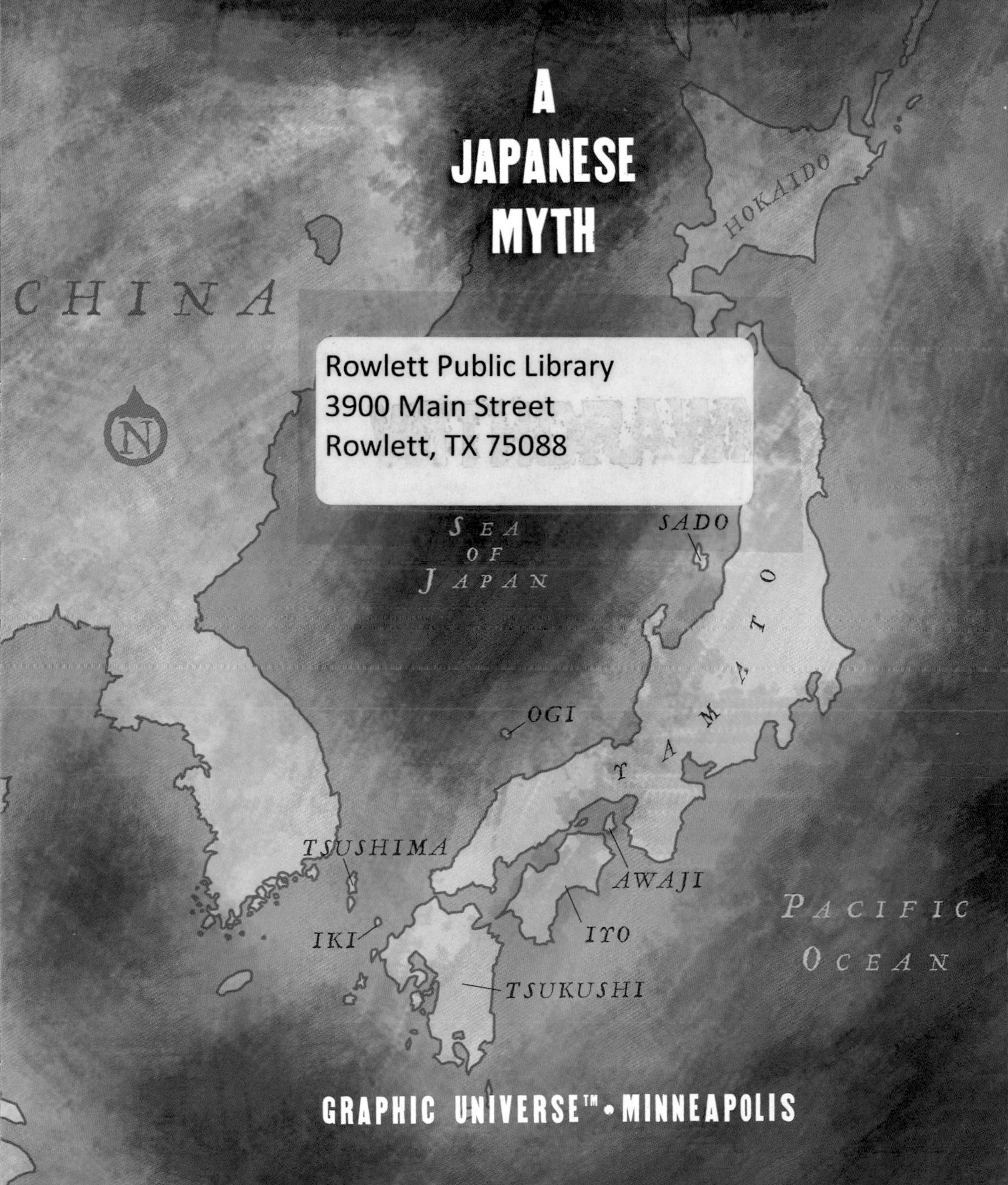

CHINA
N
SEA OF JAPAN
SADO
YAMATO
OGI
TSUSHIMA
AWAJI
IKI
ITO
TSUKUSHI
HOKAIDO
PACIFIC OCEAN

GRAPHIC UNIVERSE™ • MINNEAPOLIS

THE GODS AND GODDESSES PORTRAYED IN *AMATERASU: RETURN OF THE SUN* BELONG TO SHINTO, JAPAN'S NATIVE RELIGION. SHINTO DOES NOT HAVE SCRIPTURES OR HOLY BOOKS, BUT IT IS EXPRESSED IN ITS ANCIENT TRADITIONS, ITS MYTHOLOGY, AND ITS FOLK BELIEFS. THROUGHOUT JAPAN, SHINTO SHRINES SERVE AS HOMES TO THE SPIRITS OF GODS AND GODDESSES. THE SHRINES ARE REGULARLY VISITED BY MILLIONS OF JAPANESE PEOPLE. ONE OF JAPAN'S MOST SACRED SHRINES IS THE INNER SHRINE AT ISE JINGU IN CENTRAL HONSHU. THE INNER SHRINE IS DEDICATED TO AMATERASU, THE SHINTO GODDESS OF THE SUN. THE SHRINE HOUSES THREE ITEMS ASSOCIATED WITH AMATERASU'S STORY—A MIRROR, JEWELS, AND A SWORD.

IN ADDITION TO BRINGING LIGHT AND WARMTH TO EARTH, AS SHOWN IN THIS STORY, AMATERASU TAUGHT THE JAPANESE PEOPLE TO GROW RICE AND WHEAT, TO CULTIVATE SILKWORMS, AND TO WEAVE CLOTH ON LOOMS. FOR HUNDREDS OF YEARS, THE JAPANESE ROYAL FAMILY TRACED ITS BEGINNINGS TO AMATERASU. TO THIS DAY, SHE IS HONORED IN FESTIVALS AND STREET PROCESSIONS THROUGHOUT JAPAN EVERY JULY 17 AND DECEMBER 21.

STORY BY PAUL D. STORRIE

PENCILS AND INKS BY RON RANDALL

COLORING BY HI-FI DESIGN

LETTERING BY BILL HAUSER

CONSULTANT: YUIKO KIMURA, MINNEAPOLIS INSTITUTE OF ARTS

Thanks to Motoko Oshino and the staff at the Japan Foreign-Rights Centre in Tokyo for invaluable help with the pronunciation key.

Copyright © 2007 by Lerner Publishing Group, Inc.

Graphic Universe™ is a trademark of Lerner Publishing Group, Inc.

All rights reserved. International copyright secured. No part of this book may be reproduced, stored in a retrieval system, or transmitted in any form or by any means—electronic, mechanical, photocopying, recording, or otherwise—without the prior written permission of Lerner Publishing Group, Inc., except for the inclusion of brief quotations in an acknowledged review.

Graphic Universe™
An imprint of Lerner Publishing Group, Inc.
241 First Avenue North
Minneapolis, MN 55401 USA

For reading levels and more information, look up this title at www.lernerbooks.com.

Library of Congress Cataloging-in-Publication Data

Storrie, Paul D.
Amaterasu: return of the sun / story by Paul D. Storrie; pencils and inks by Ron Randall.
    p.   cm. — (Graphic myths and legends)
    Includes index.
    ISBN 978-0-8225-5968-9 (lib. bdg. : alk. paper)
    ISBN 978-0-8225-8789-7 (EB pdf)
    1. Mythology, Japanese—Juvenile literature.
    2. Amaterasu Omikami (Shinto deity)—Juvenile literature. I. Randall, Ron. II. Title. III. Series.
    BL2203.S76   2007
    299.5'6113—dc22   2006006052

Manufactured in the United States of America
5-43493-5167-1/3/2017

TABLE OF CONTENTS

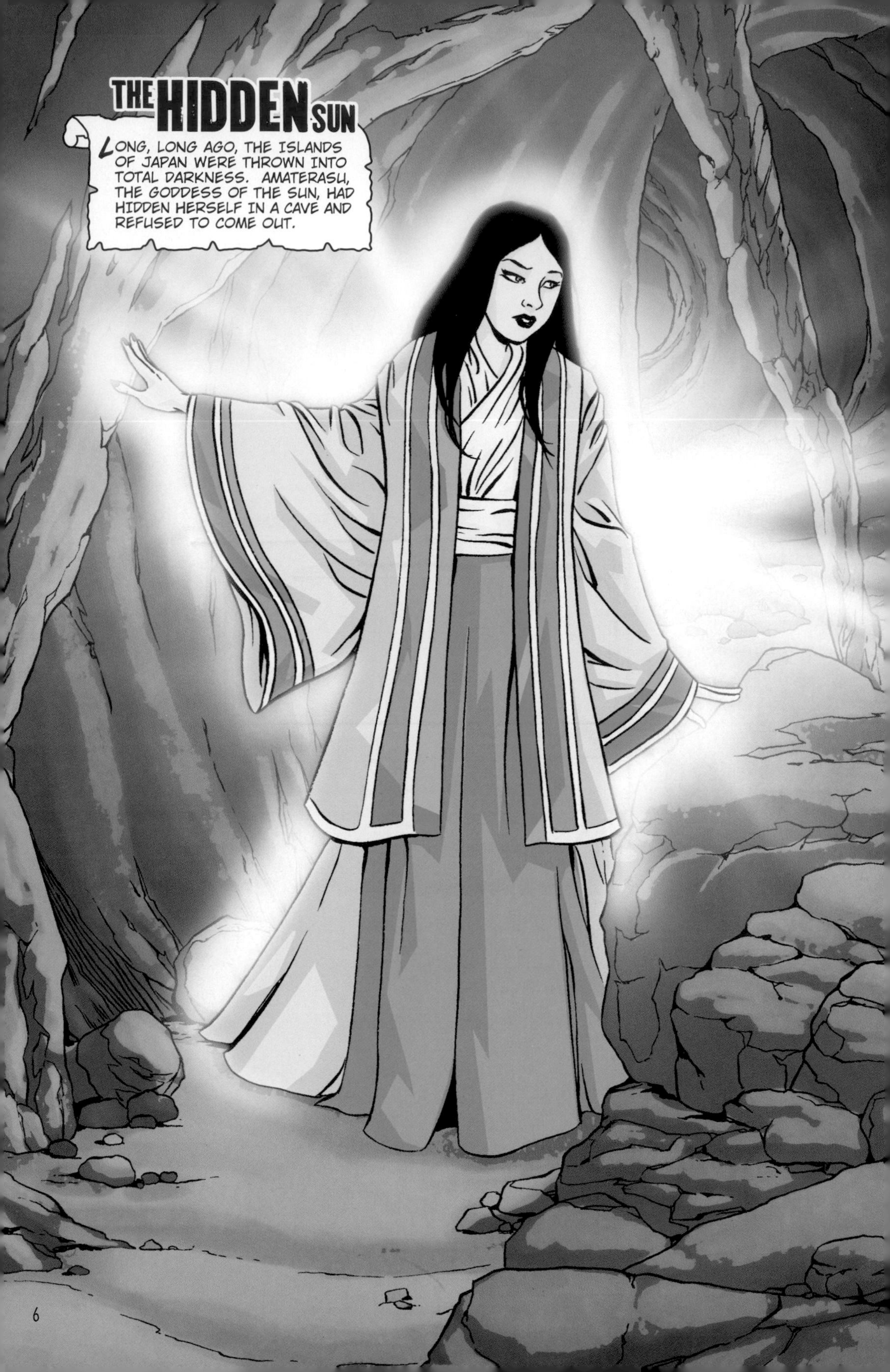
THE HIDDEN SUN
LONG, LONG AGO, THE ISLANDS OF JAPAN WERE THROWN INTO TOTAL DARKNESS. AMATERASU, THE GODDESS OF THE SUN, HAD HIDDEN HERSELF IN A CAVE AND REFUSED TO COME OUT.

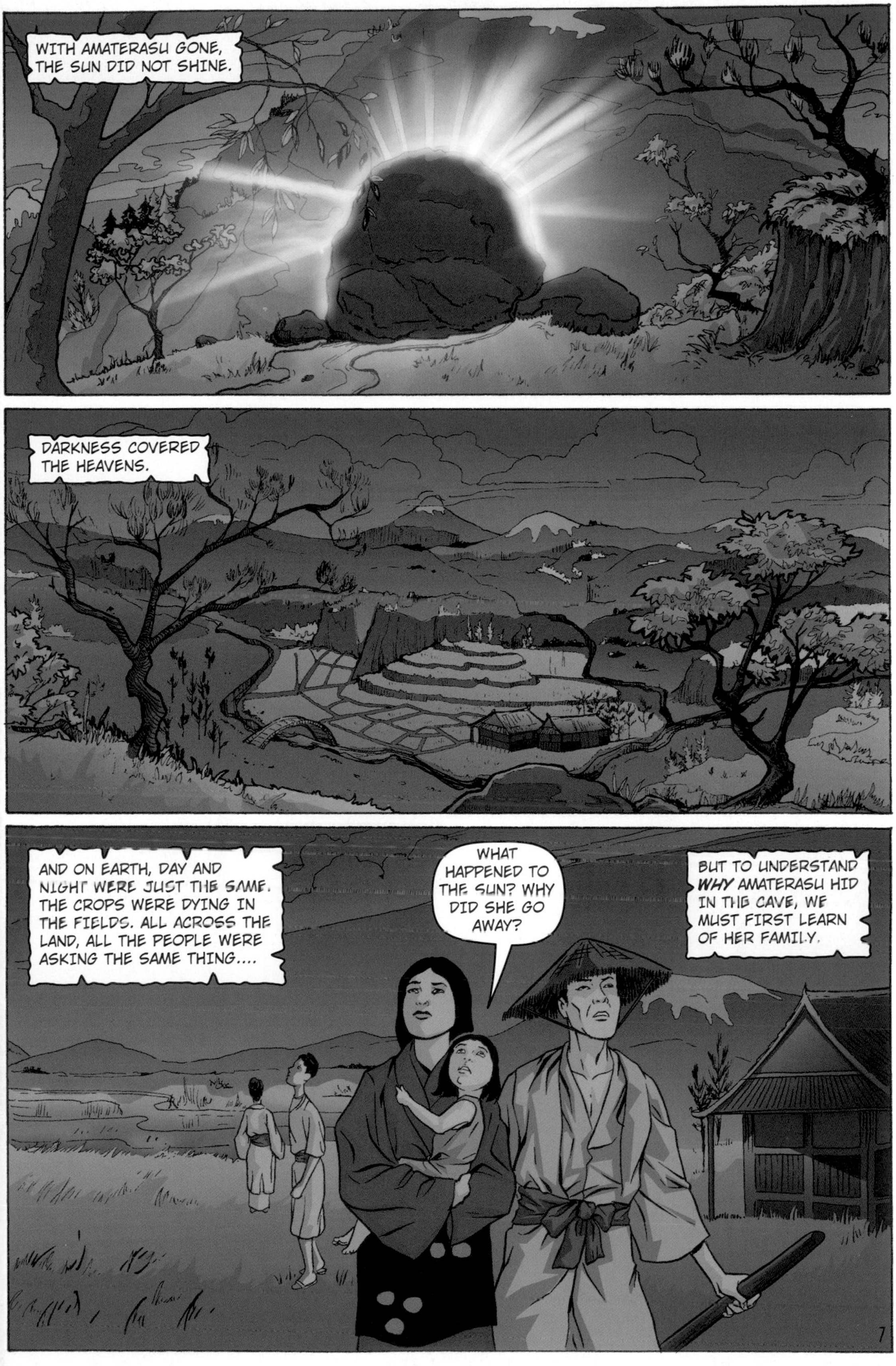
WITH AMATERASU GONE, THE SUN DID NOT SHINE.
DARKNESS COVERED THE HEAVENS.
AND ON EARTH, DAY AND NIGHT WERE JUST THE SAME. THE CROPS WERE DYING IN THE FIELDS. ALL ACROSS THE LAND, ALL THE PEOPLE WERE ASKING THE SAME THING....
WHAT HAPPENED TO THE SUN? WHY DID SHE GO AWAY?
BUT TO UNDERSTAND ***WHY*** AMATERASU HID IN THE CAVE, WE MUST FIRST LEARN OF HER FAMILY.

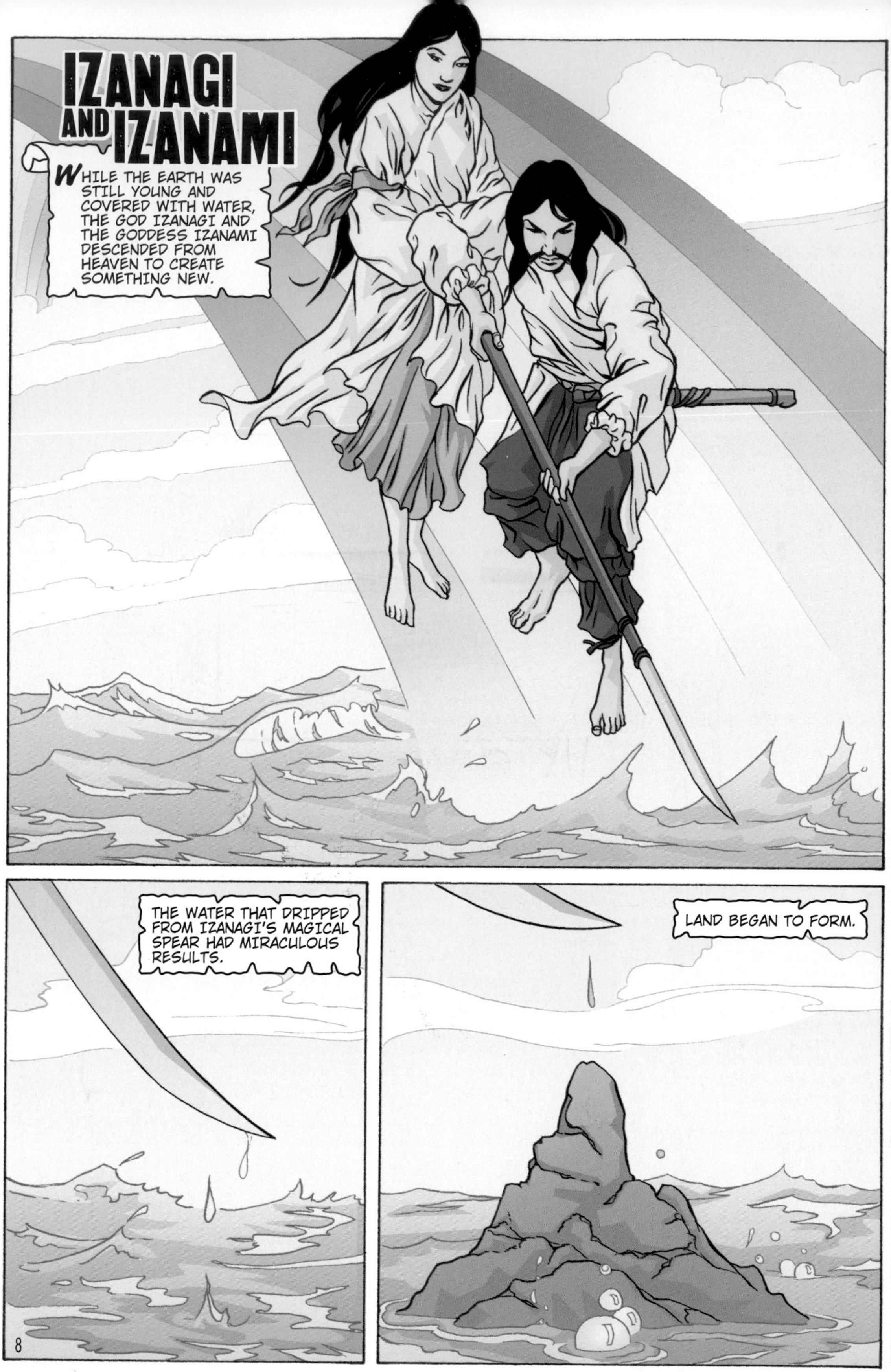
IZANAGI AND IZANAMI
WHILE THE EARTH WAS STILL YOUNG AND COVERED WITH WATER, THE GOD IZANAGI AND THE GODDESS IZANAMI DESCENDED FROM HEAVEN TO CREATE SOMETHING NEW.
THE WATER THAT DRIPPED FROM IZANAGI'S MAGICAL SPEAR HAD MIRACULOUS RESULTS.
LAND BEGAN TO FORM.

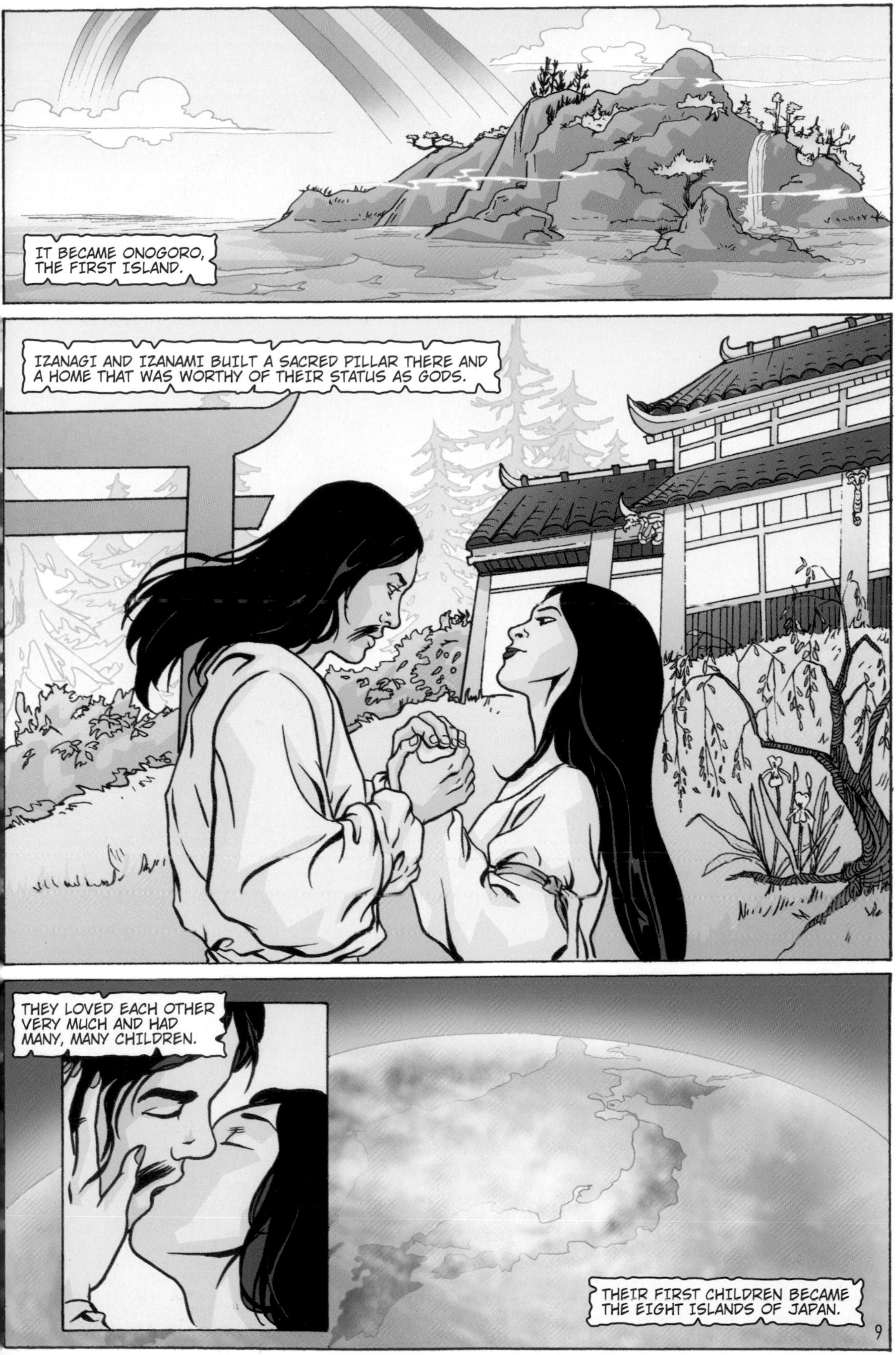
IT BECAME ONOGORO, THE FIRST ISLAND.
IZANAGI AND IZANAMI BUILT A SACRED PILLAR THERE AND A HOME THAT WAS WORTHY OF THEIR STATUS AS GODS.
THEY LOVED EACH OTHER VERY MUCH AND HAD MANY, MANY CHILDREN.
THEIR FIRST CHILDREN BECAME THE EIGHT ISLANDS OF JAPAN.

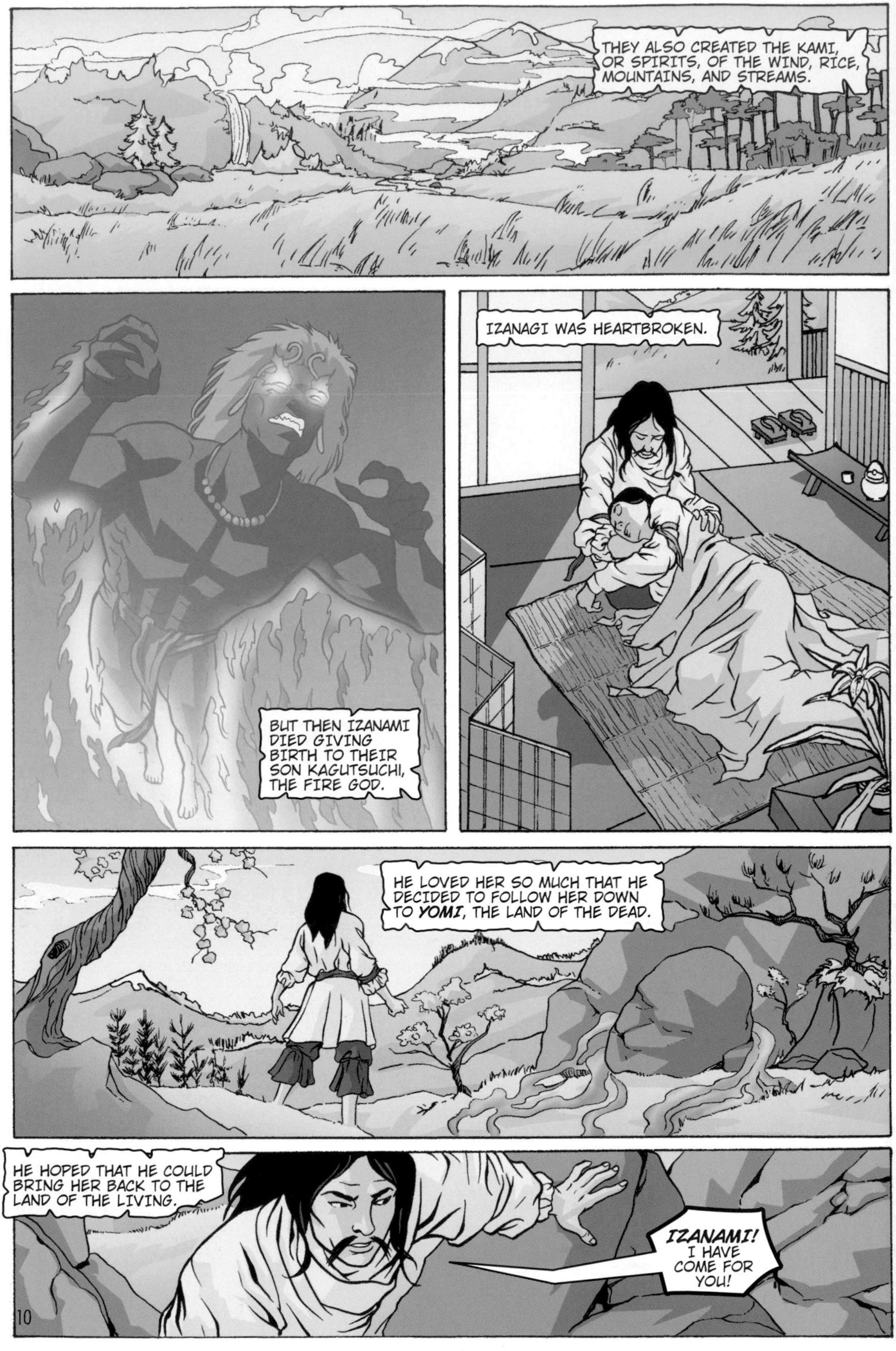
THEY ALSO CREATED THE KAMI, OR SPIRITS, OF THE WIND, RICE, MOUNTAINS, AND STREAMS.
BUT THEN IZANAMI DIED GIVING BIRTH TO THEIR SON KAGUTSUCHI, THE FIRE GOD.
IZANAGI WAS HEARTBROKEN.
HE LOVED HER SO MUCH THAT HE DECIDED TO FOLLOW HER DOWN TO *YOMI*, THE LAND OF THE DEAD.
HE HOPED THAT HE COULD BRING HER BACK TO THE LAND OF THE LIVING.
IZANAMI! I HAVE COME FOR YOU!

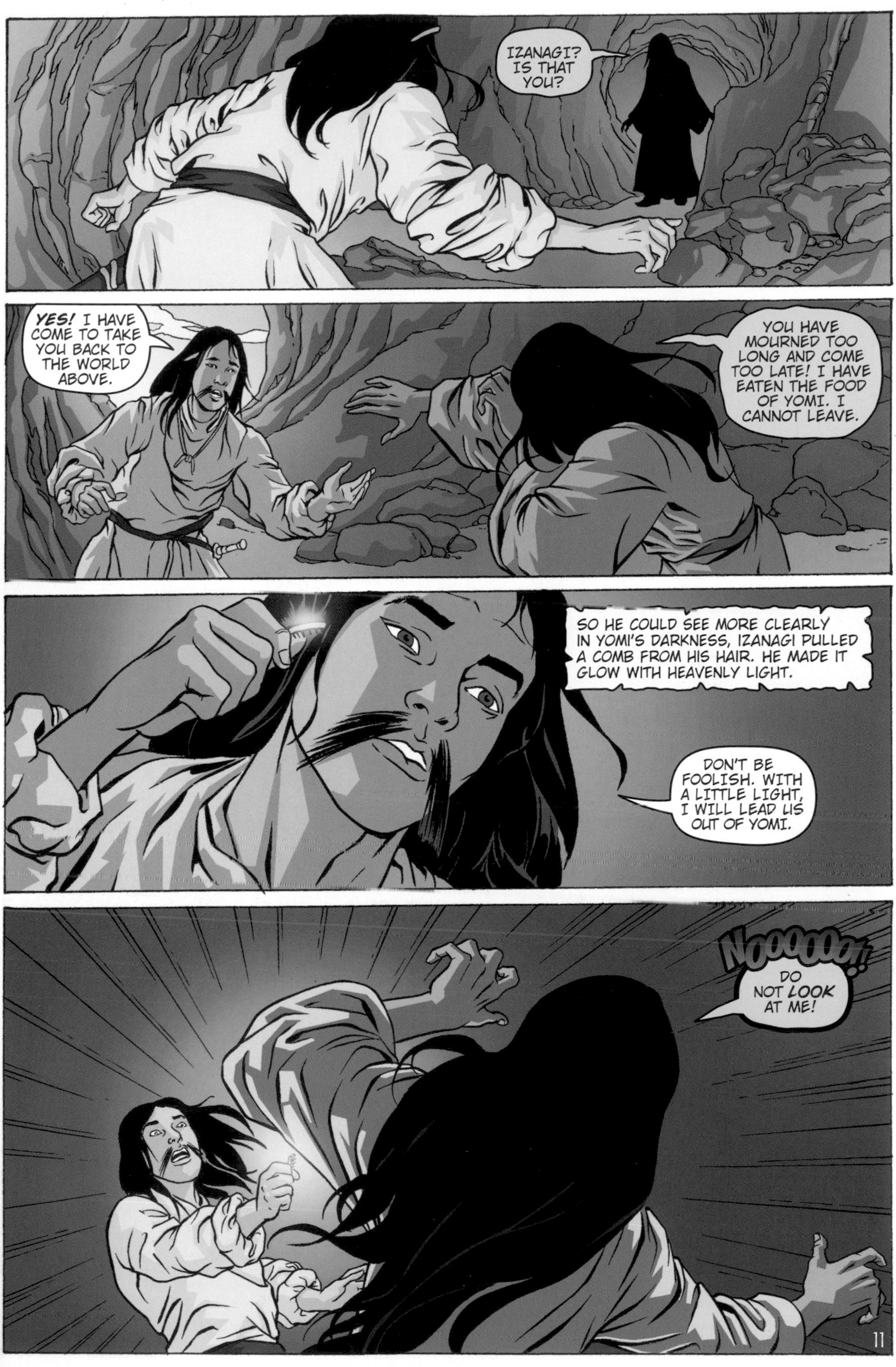
IZANAGI? IS THAT YOU?
YES! I HAVE COME TO TAKE YOU BACK TO THE WORLD ABOVE.
YOU HAVE MOURNED TOO LONG AND COME TOO LATE! I HAVE EATEN THE FOOD OF YOMI. I CANNOT LEAVE.
SO HE COULD SEE MORE CLEARLY IN YOMI'S DARKNESS, IZANAGI PULLED A COMB FROM HIS HAIR. HE MADE IT GLOW WITH HEAVENLY LIGHT.
DON'T BE FOOLISH. WITH A LITTLE LIGHT, I WILL LEAD US OUT OF YOMI.
NOOOOOO!
DO NOT LOOK AT ME!
11

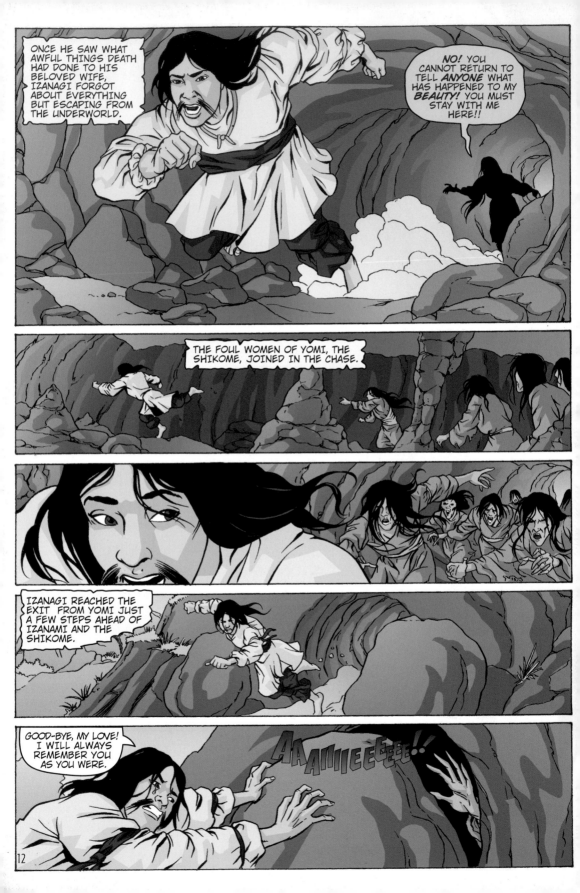

ONCE HE SAW WHAT AWFUL THINGS DEATH HAD DONE TO HIS BELOVED WIFE, IZANAGI FORGOT ABOUT EVERYTHING BUT ESCAPING FROM THE UNDERWORLD.

NO! YOU CANNOT RETURN TO TELL *ANYONE* WHAT HAS HAPPENED TO MY *BEAUTY!* YOU MUST STAY WITH ME HERE!!

THE FOUL WOMEN OF YOMI, THE SHIKOME, JOINED IN THE CHASE.

IZANAGI REACHED THE EXIT FROM YOMI JUST A FEW STEPS AHEAD OF IZANAMI AND THE SHIKOME.

GOOD-BYE, MY LOVE! I WILL ALWAYS REMEMBER YOU AS YOU WERE.

AAAIIIEEEEEE...

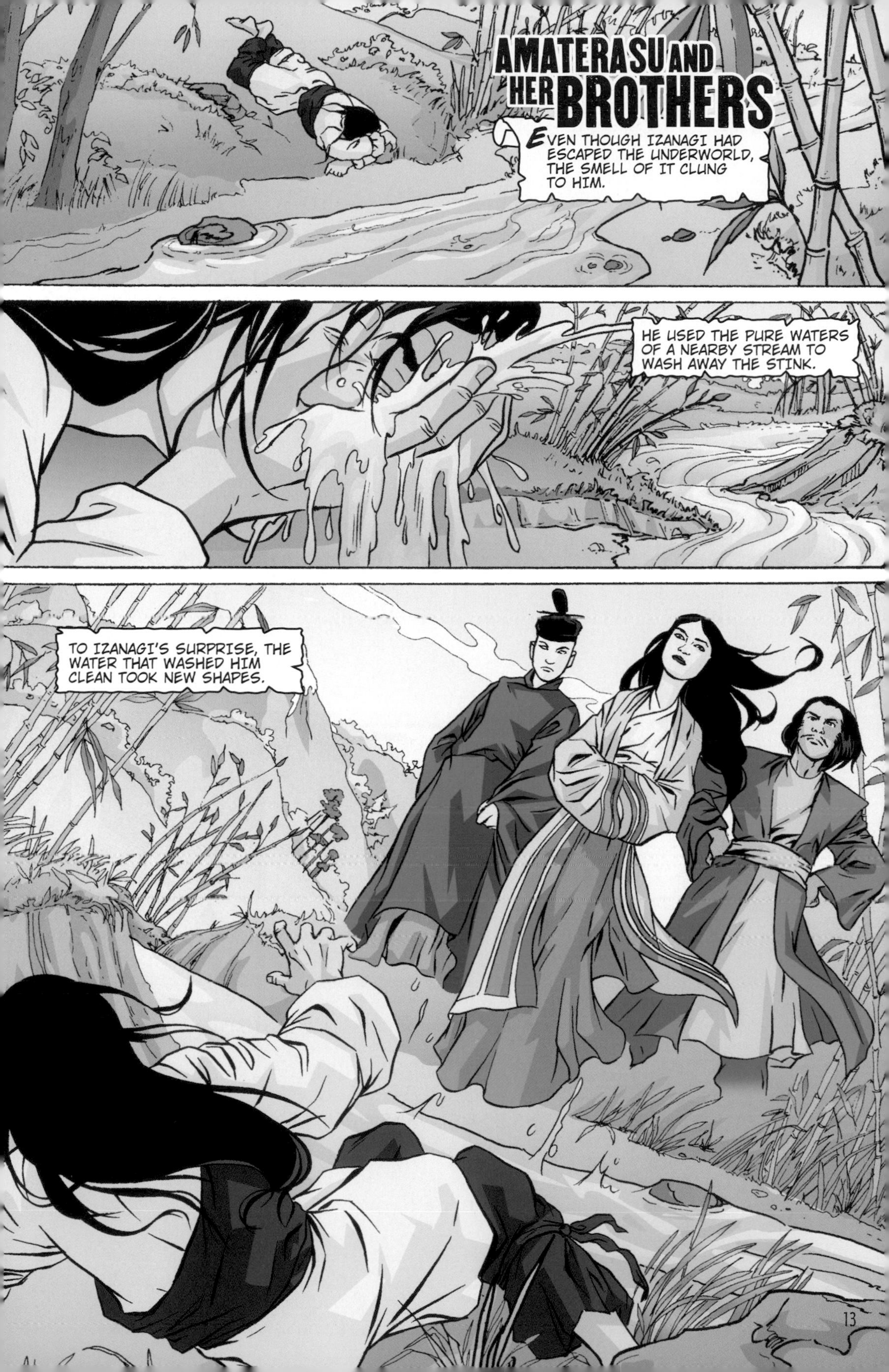
AMATERASU AND HER BROTHERS
EVEN THOUGH IZANAGI HAD ESCAPED THE UNDERWORLD, THE SMELL OF IT CLUNG TO HIM.
HE USED THE PURE WATERS OF A NEARBY STREAM TO WASH AWAY THE STINK.
TO IZANAGI'S SURPRISE, THE WATER THAT WASHED HIM CLEAN TOOK NEW SHAPES.

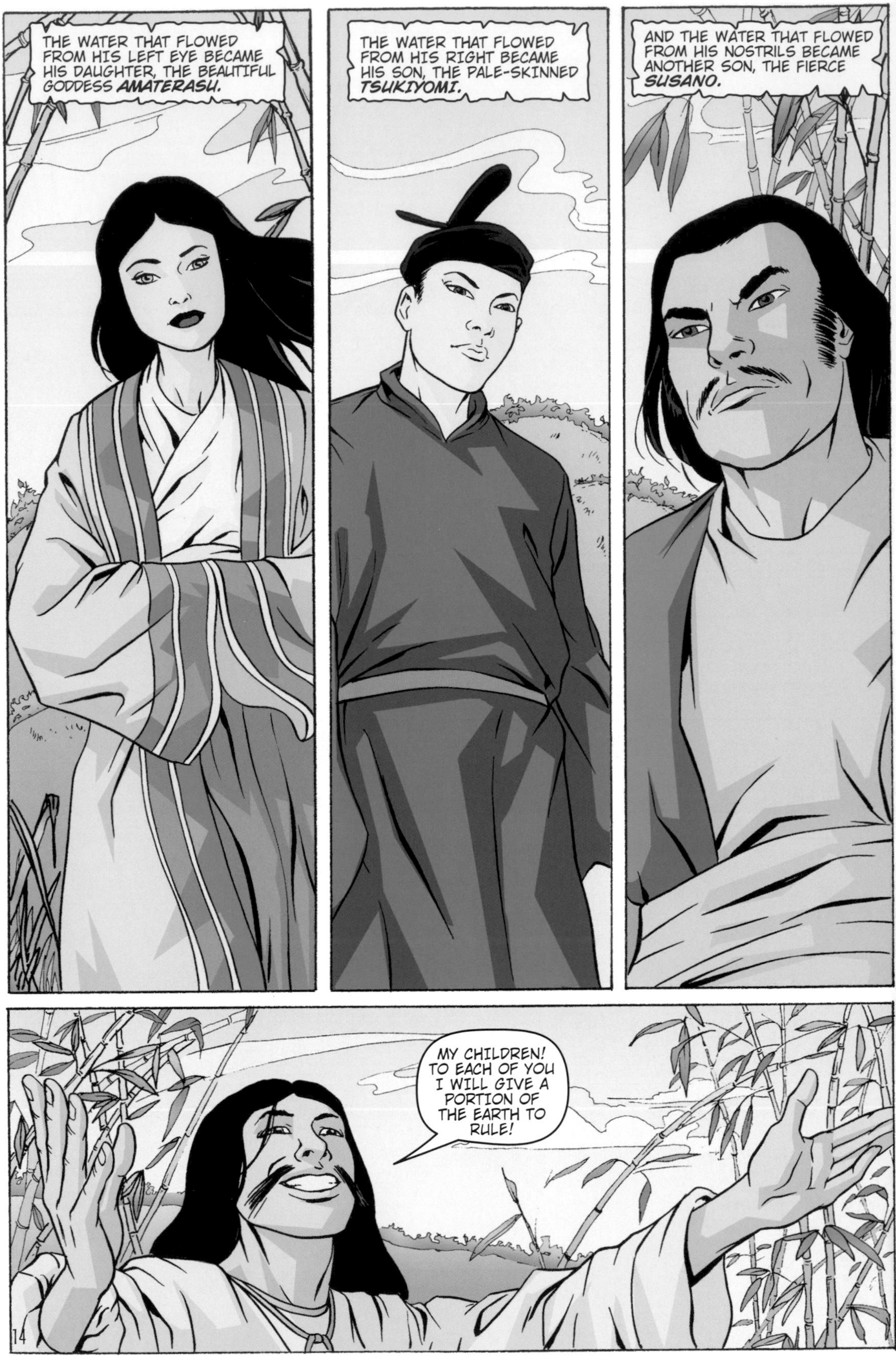
THE WATER THAT FLOWED FROM HIS LEFT EYE BECAME HIS DAUGHTER, THE BEAUTIFUL GODDESS AMATERASU.
THE WATER THAT FLOWED FROM HIS RIGHT BECAME HIS SON, THE PALE-SKINNED TSUKIYOMI.
AND THE WATER THAT FLOWED FROM HIS NOSTRILS BECAME ANOTHER SON, THE FIERCE SUSANO.
MY CHILDREN! TO EACH OF YOU I WILL GIVE A PORTION OF THE EARTH TO RULE!

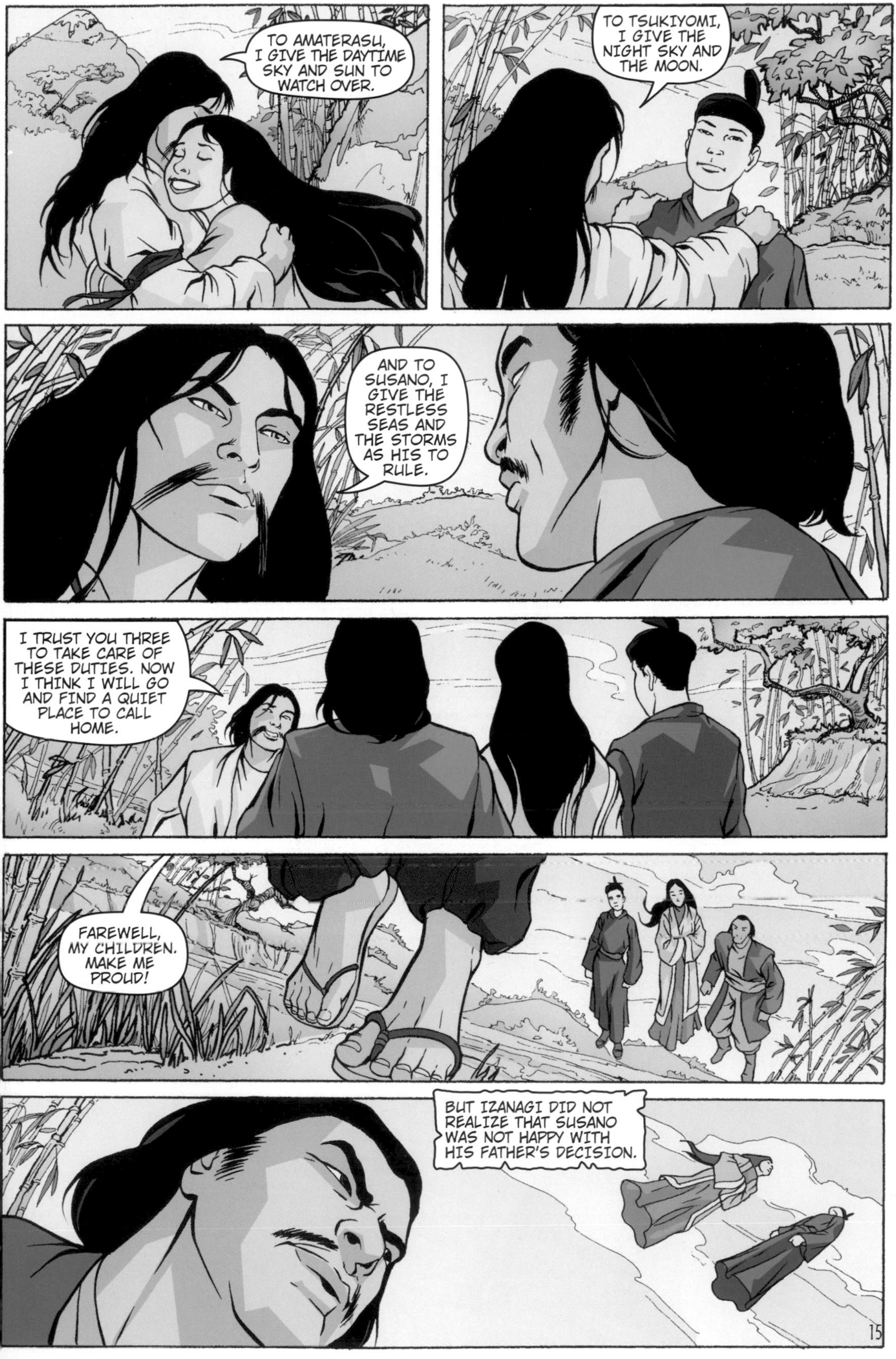
TO AMATERASU, I GIVE THE DAYTIME SKY AND SUN TO WATCH OVER.
TO TSUKIYOMI, I GIVE THE NIGHT SKY AND THE MOON.
AND TO SUSANO, I GIVE THE RESTLESS SEAS AND THE STORMS AS HIS TO RULE.
I TRUST YOU THREE TO TAKE CARE OF THESE DUTIES. NOW I THINK I WILL GO AND FIND A QUIET PLACE TO CALL HOME.
FAREWELL, MY CHILDREN. MAKE ME PROUD!
BUT IZANAGI DID NOT REALIZE THAT SUSANO WAS NOT HAPPY WITH HIS FATHER'S DECISION.

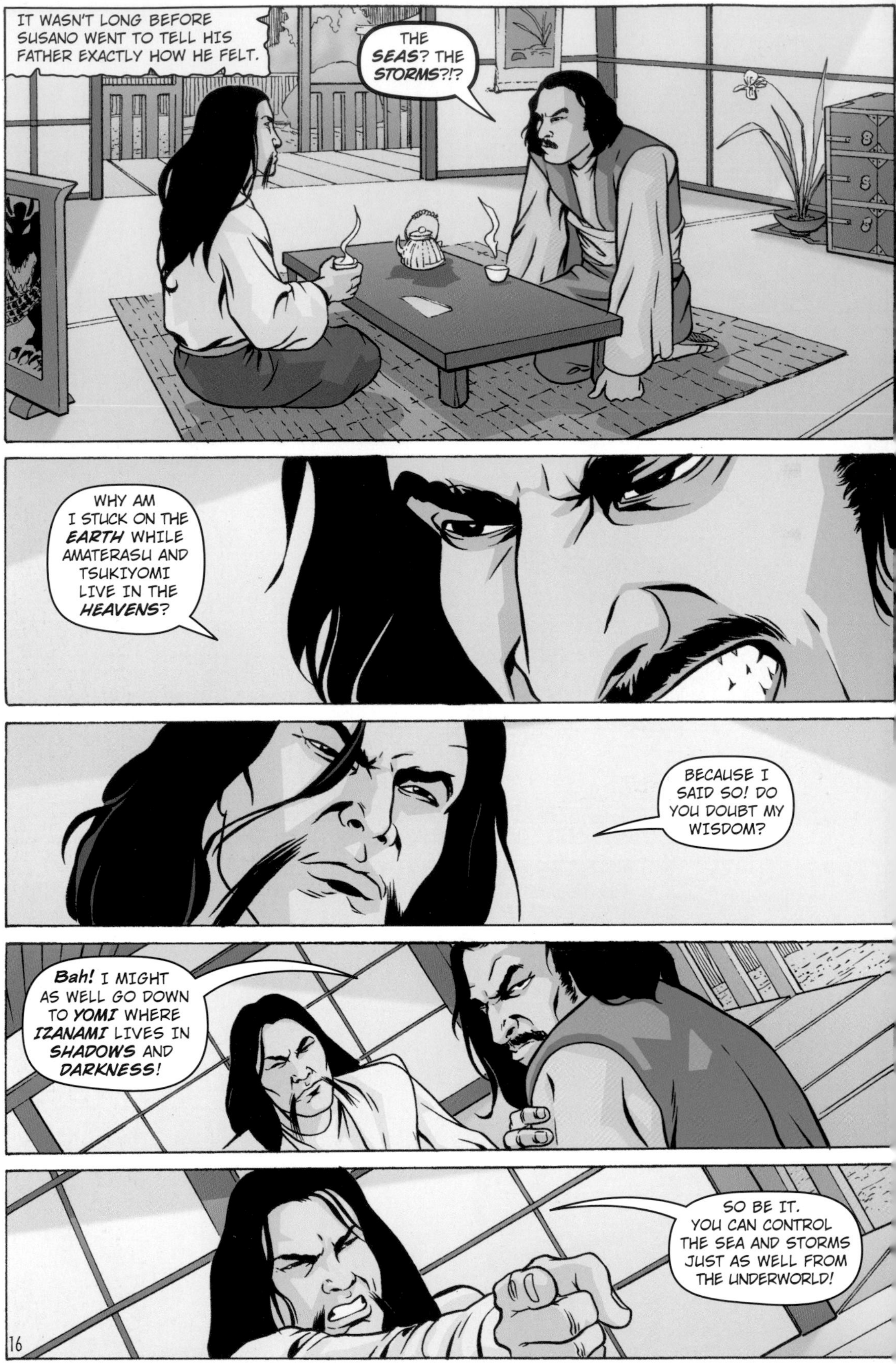
IT WASN'T LONG BEFORE SUSANO WENT TO TELL HIS FATHER EXACTLY HOW HE FELT.
THE SEAS? THE STORMS?!?
WHY AM I STUCK ON THE EARTH WHILE AMATERASU AND TSUKIYOMI LIVE IN THE HEAVENS?
BECAUSE I SAID SO! DO YOU DOUBT MY WISDOM?
Bah! I MIGHT AS WELL GO DOWN TO YOMI WHERE IZANAMI LIVES IN SHADOWS AND DARKNESS!
SO BE IT. YOU CAN CONTROL THE SEA AND STORMS JUST AS WELL FROM THE UNDERWORLD!

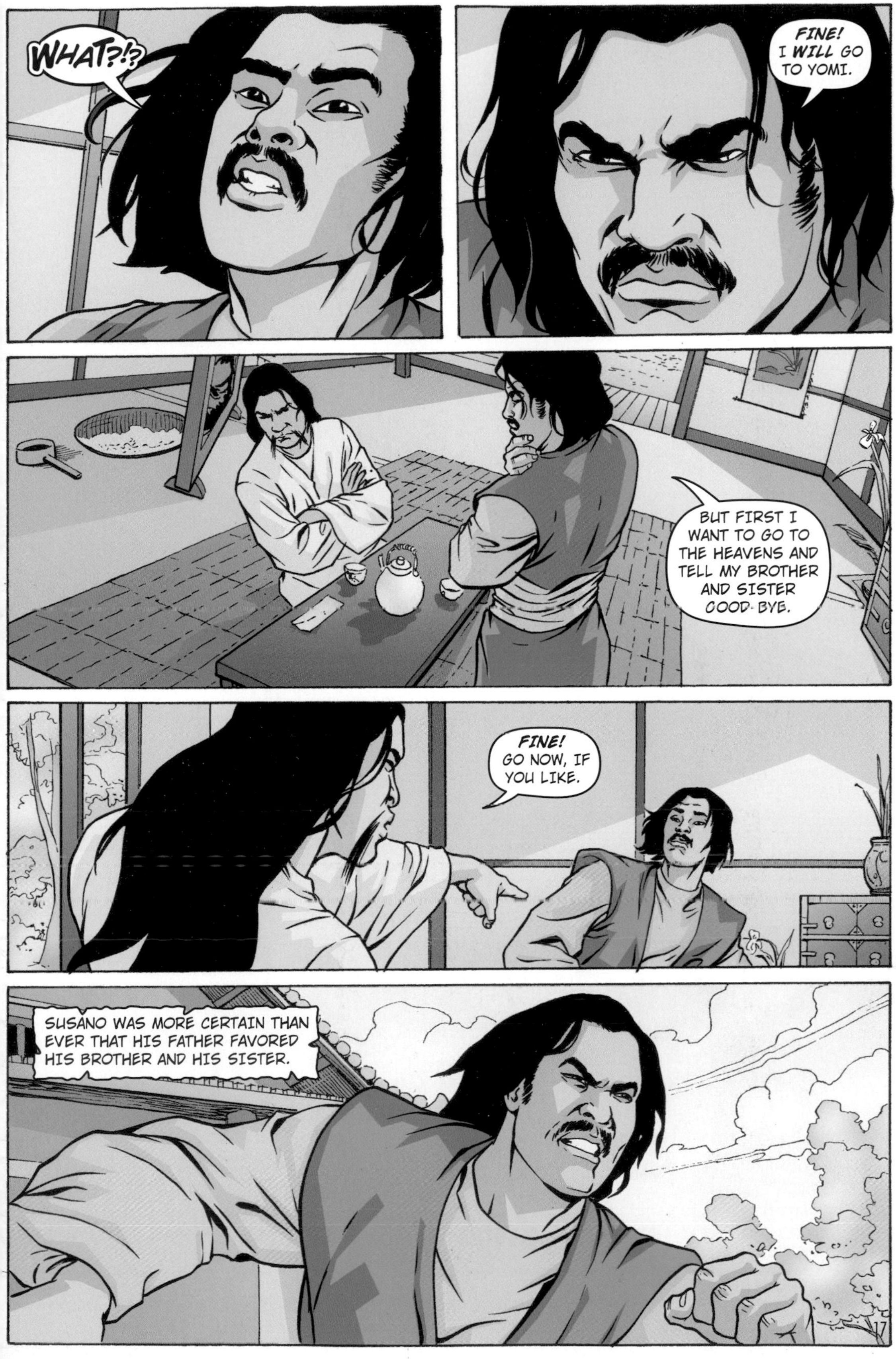
WHAT?!?
FINE! I WILL GO TO YOMI.
BUT FIRST I WANT TO GO TO THE HEAVENS AND TELL MY BROTHER AND SISTER GOOD-BYE.
FINE! GO NOW, IF YOU LIKE.
SUSANO WAS MORE CERTAIN THAN EVER THAT HIS FATHER FAVORED HIS BROTHER AND HIS SISTER.

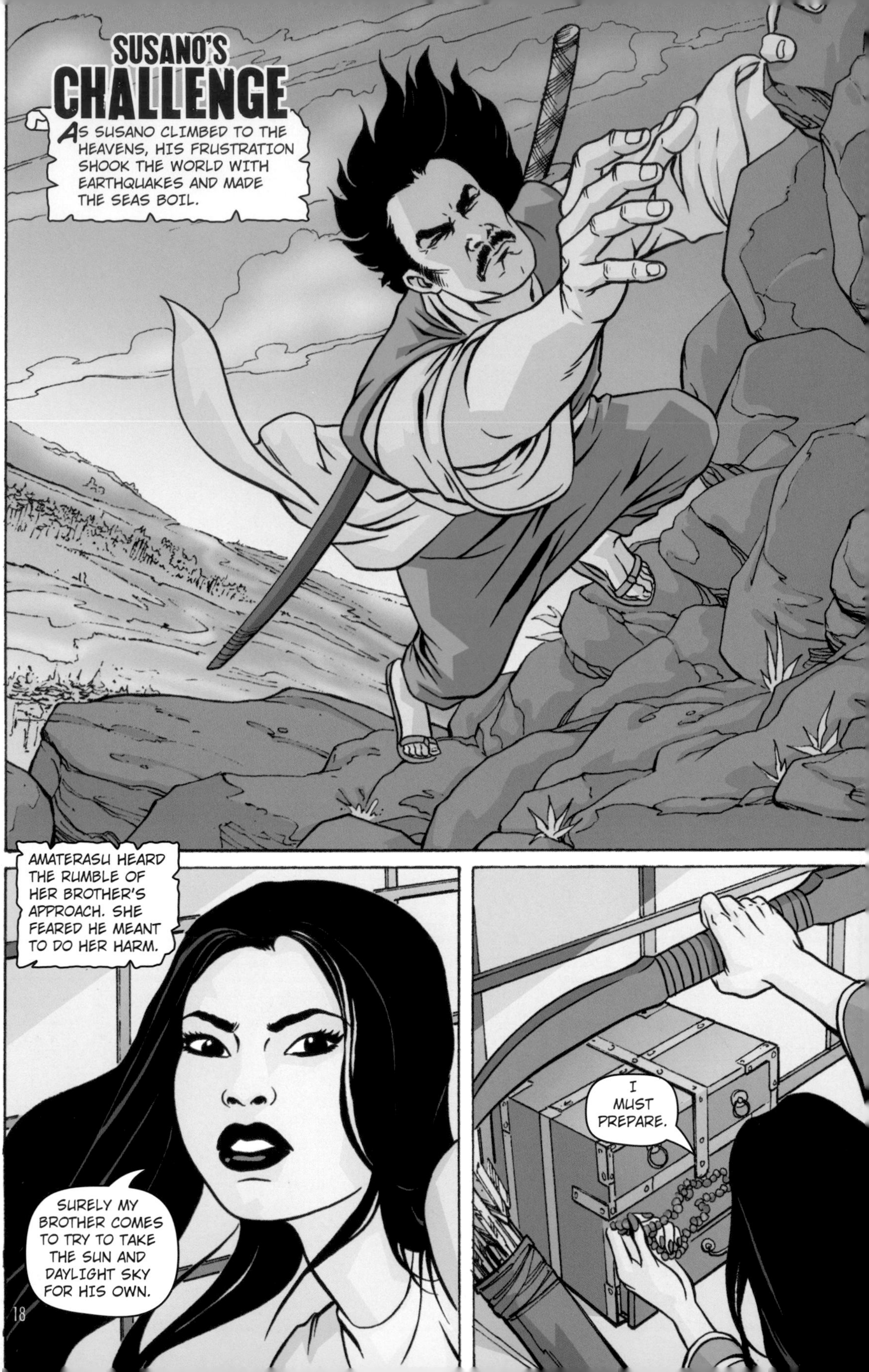
SUSANO'S CHALLENGE
AS SUSANO CLIMBED TO THE HEAVENS, HIS FRUSTRATION SHOOK THE WORLD WITH EARTHQUAKES AND MADE THE SEAS BOIL.
AMATERASU HEARD THE RUMBLE OF HER BROTHER'S APPROACH. SHE FEARED HE MEANT TO DO HER HARM.
SURELY MY BROTHER COMES TO TRY TO TAKE THE SUN AND DAYLIGHT SKY FOR HIS OWN.
I MUST PREPARE.

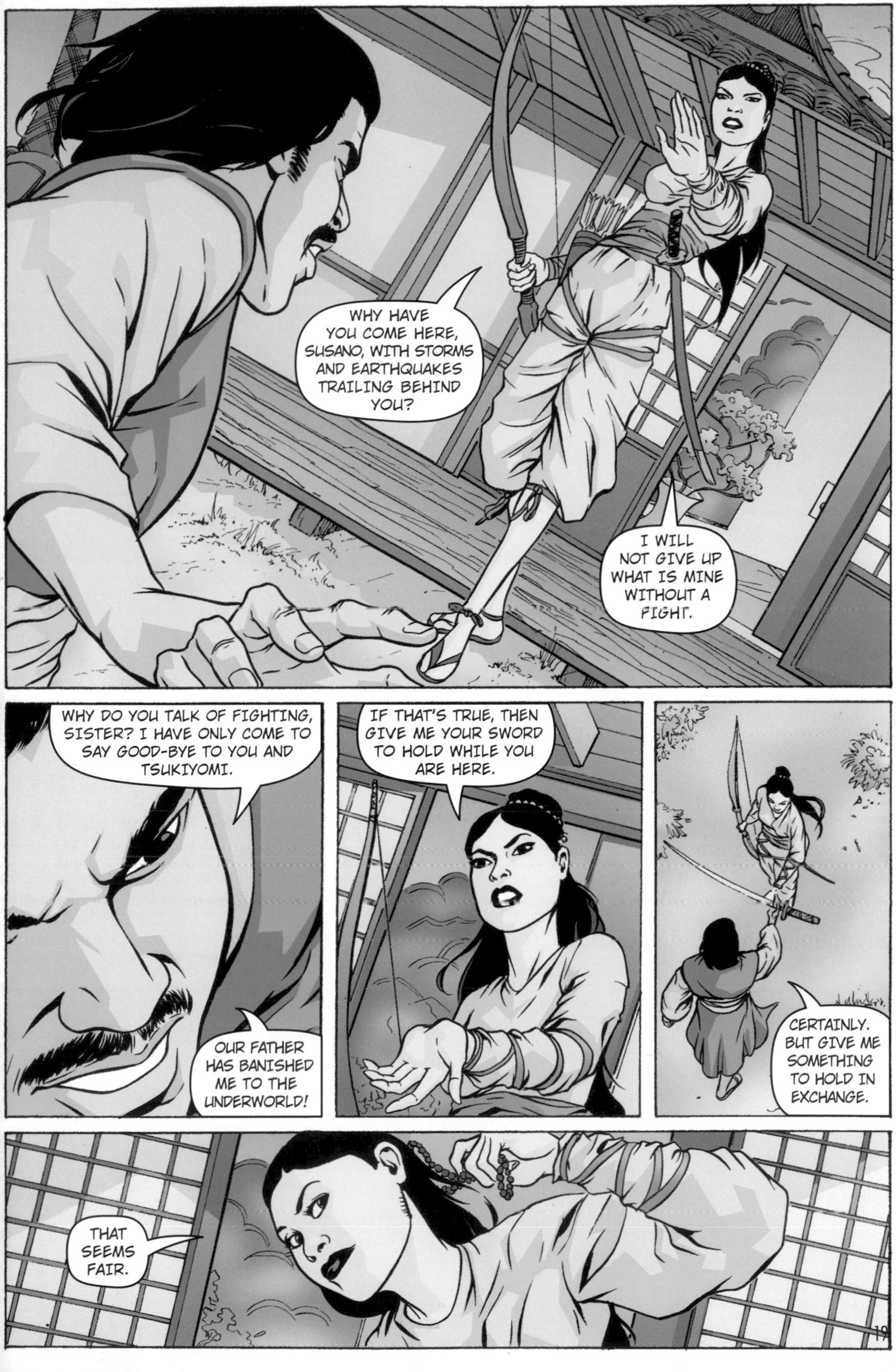
WHY HAVE YOU COME HERE, SUSANO, WITH STORMS AND EARTHQUAKES TRAILING BEHIND YOU?
I WILL NOT GIVE UP WHAT IS MINE WITHOUT A FIGHT.
WHY DO YOU TALK OF FIGHTING, SISTER? I HAVE ONLY COME TO SAY GOOD-BYE TO YOU AND TSUKIYOMI.
OUR FATHER HAS BANISHED ME TO THE UNDERWORLD!
IF THAT'S TRUE, THEN GIVE ME YOUR SWORD TO HOLD WHILE YOU ARE HERE.
CERTAINLY. BUT GIVE ME SOMETHING TO HOLD IN EXCHANGE.
THAT SEEMS FAIR.

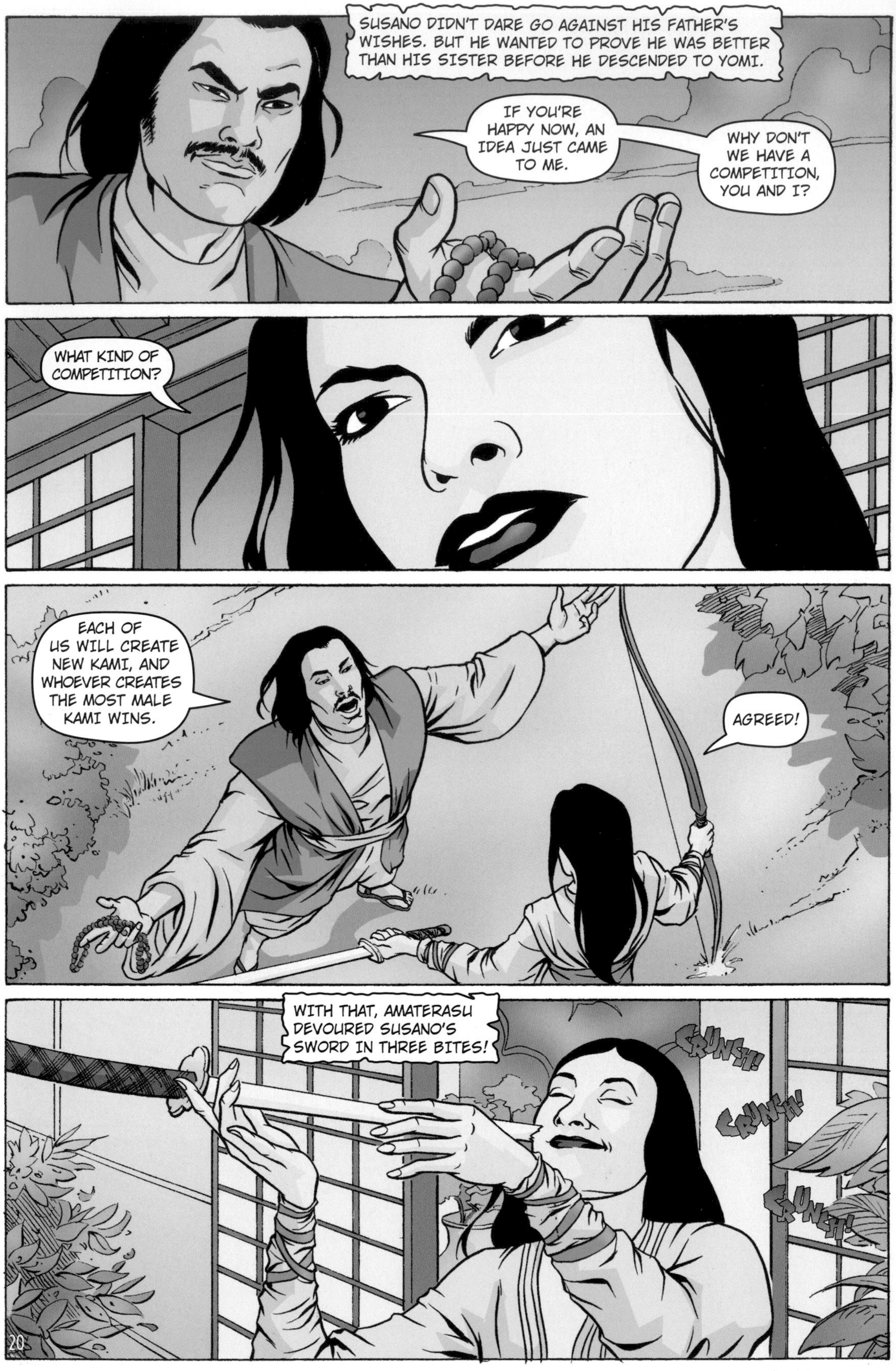
SUSANO DIDN'T DARE GO AGAINST HIS FATHER'S WISHES. BUT HE WANTED TO PROVE HE WAS BETTER THAN HIS SISTER BEFORE HE DESCENDED TO YOMI.
IF YOU'RE HAPPY NOW, AN IDEA JUST CAME TO ME.
WHY DON'T WE HAVE A COMPETITION, YOU AND I?
WHAT KIND OF COMPETITION?
EACH OF US WILL CREATE NEW KAMI, AND WHOEVER CREATES THE MOST MALE KAMI WINS.
AGREED!
WITH THAT, AMATERASU DEVOURED SUSANO'S SWORD IN THREE BITES!
CRUNCH!
CRUNCH!
CRUNCH!

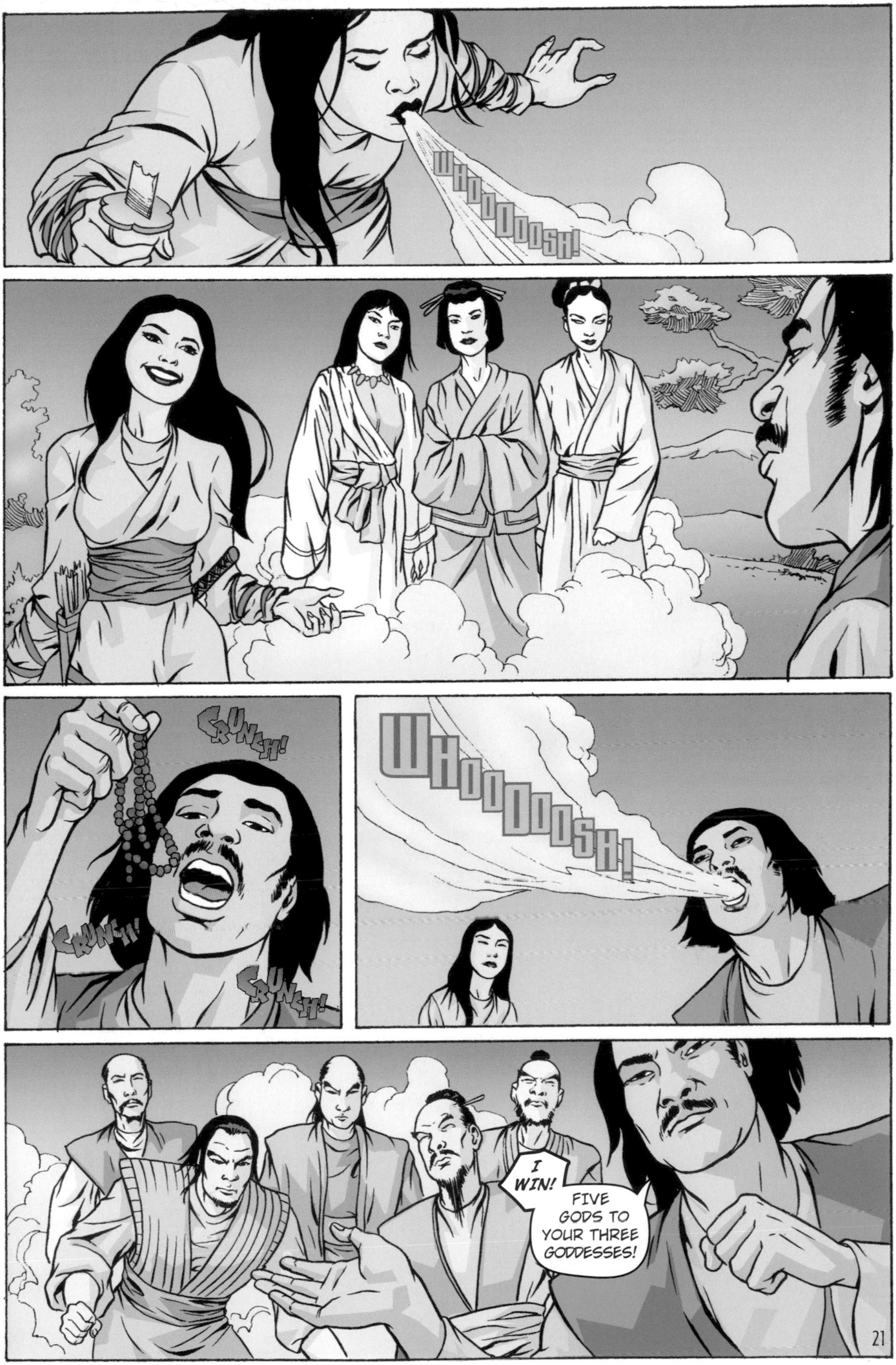
WHOOOOOOSH!
CRUNCH!
CRUNCH!
CRUNCH!
WHOOOOOOSH!
I WIN!
FIVE GODS TO YOUR THREE GODDESSES!

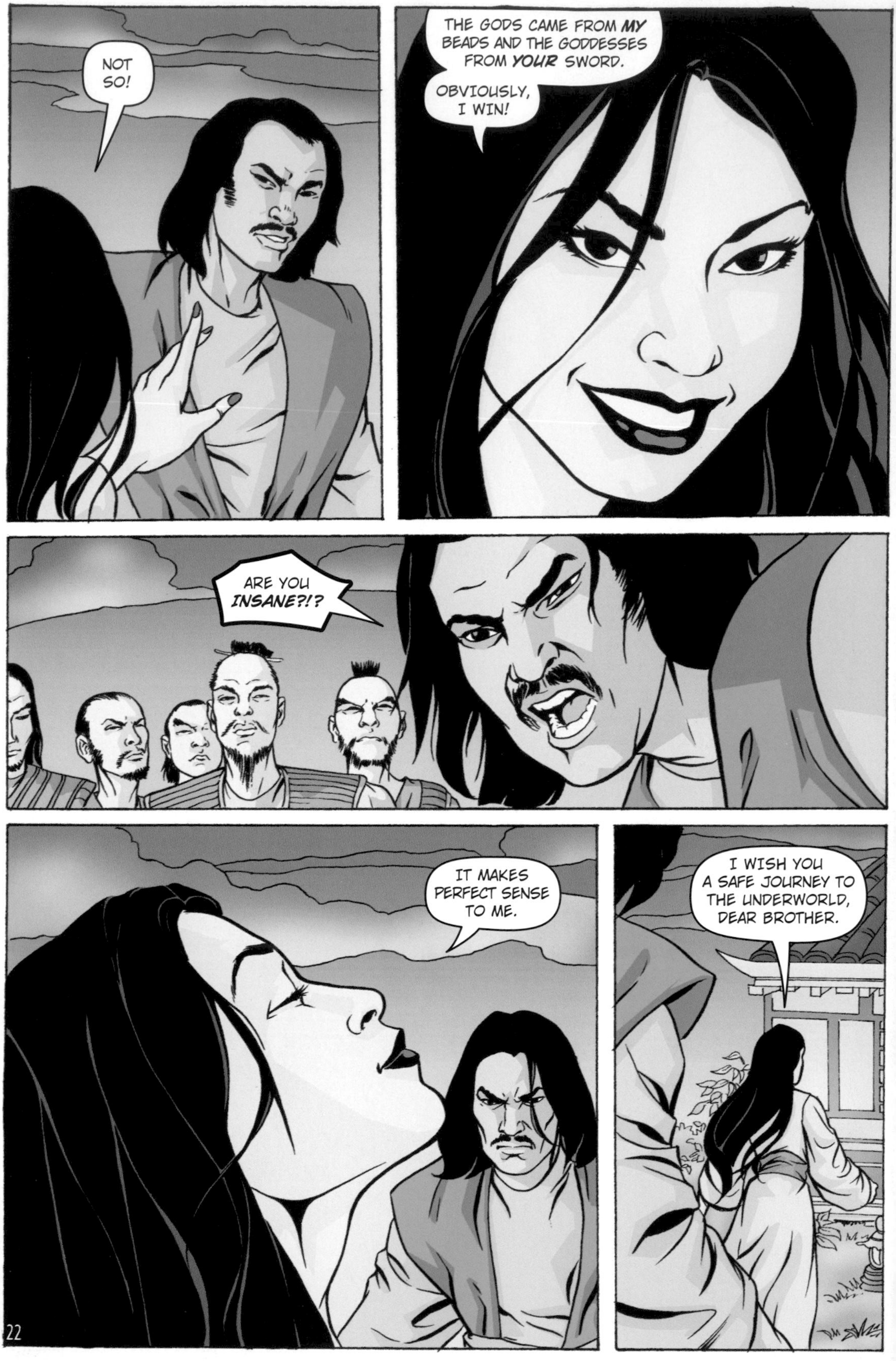
NOT SO!
THE GODS CAME FROM *MY* BEADS AND THE GODDESSES FROM *YOUR* SWORD.
OBVIOUSLY, I WIN!
ARE YOU *INSANE?!?*
IT MAKES PERFECT SENSE TO ME.
I WISH YOU A SAFE JOURNEY TO THE UNDERWORLD, DEAR BROTHER.

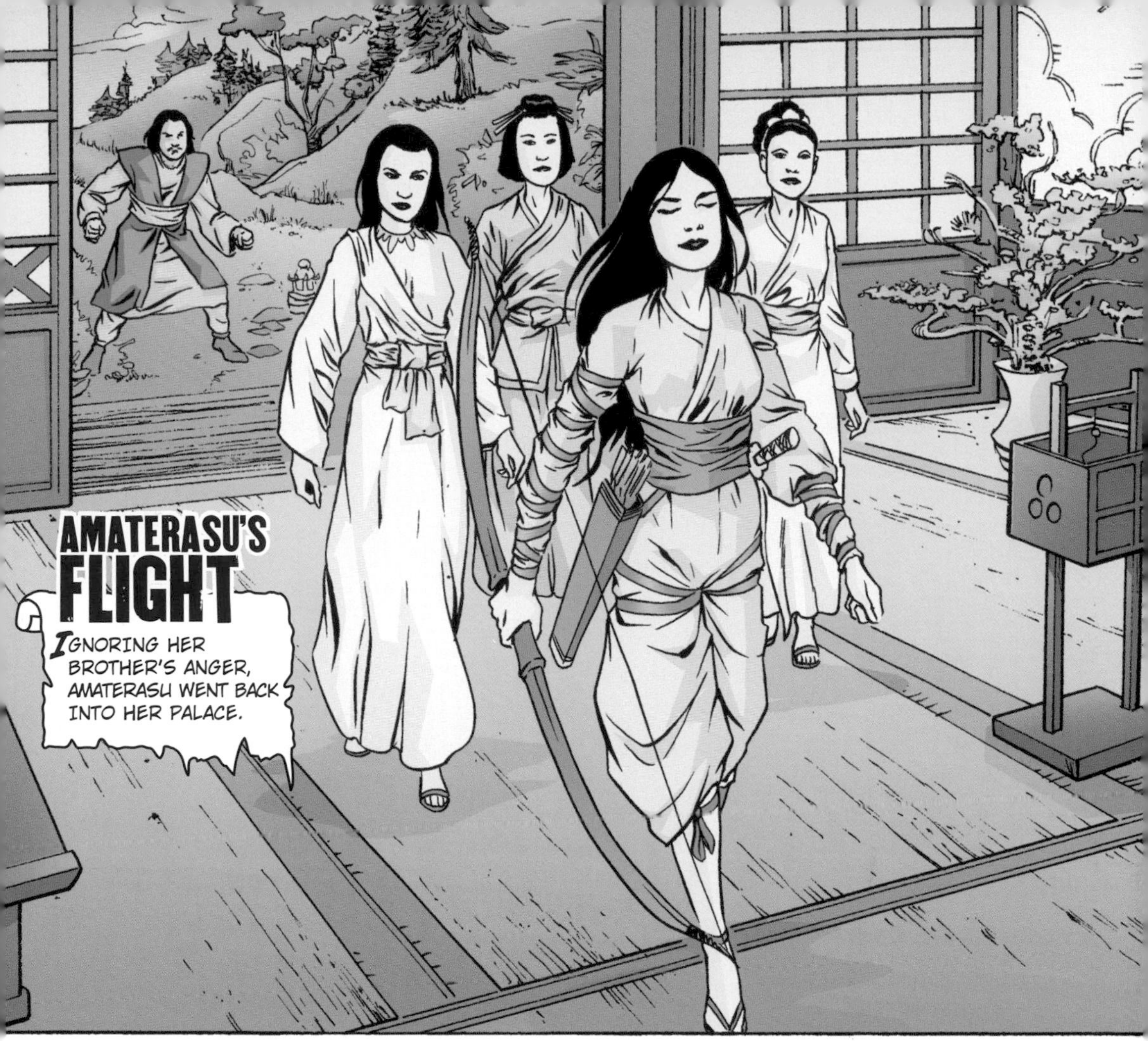
AMATERASU'S FLIGHT
IGNORING HER BROTHER'S ANGER, AMATERASU WENT BACK INTO HER PALACE.

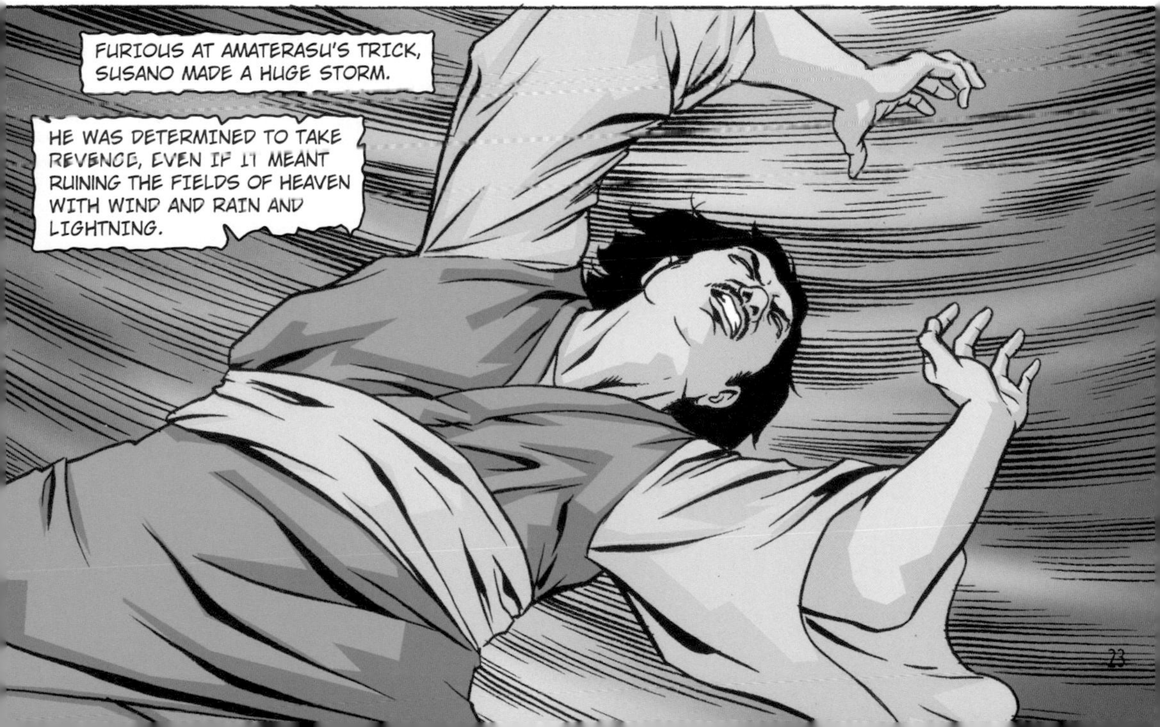
FURIOUS AT AMATERASU'S TRICK, SUSANO MADE A HUGE STORM.
HE WAS DETERMINED TO TAKE REVENGE, EVEN IF IT MEANT RUINING THE FIELDS OF HEAVEN WITH WIND AND RAIN AND LIGHTNING.

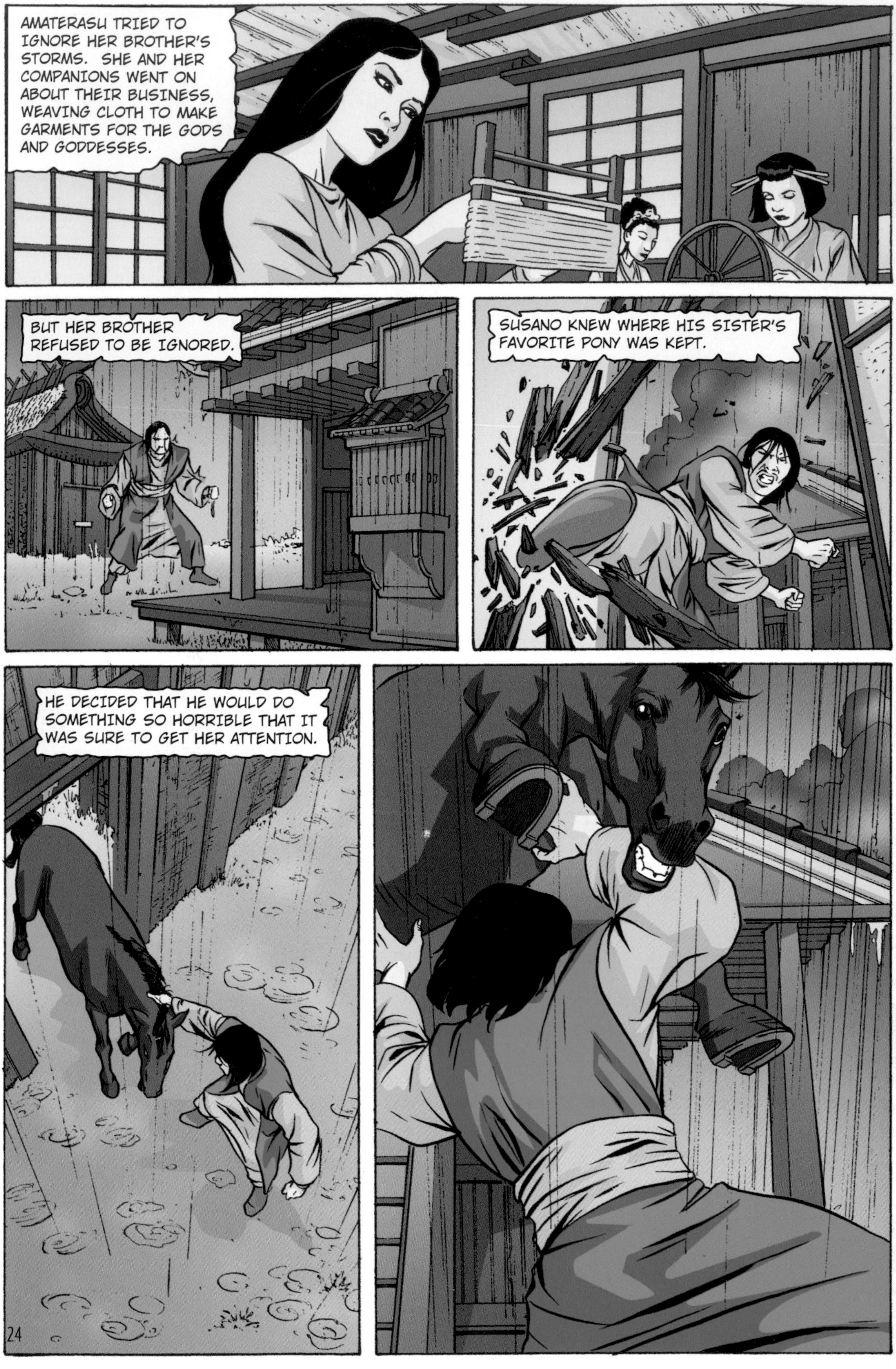
AMATERASU TRIED TO IGNORE HER BROTHER'S STORMS. SHE AND HER COMPANIONS WENT ON ABOUT THEIR BUSINESS, WEAVING CLOTH TO MAKE GARMENTS FOR THE GODS AND GODDESSES.
BUT HER BROTHER REFUSED TO BE IGNORED.
SUSANO KNEW WHERE HIS SISTER'S FAVORITE PONY WAS KEPT.
HE DECIDED THAT HE WOULD DO SOMETHING SO HORRIBLE THAT IT WAS SURE TO GET HER ATTENTION.

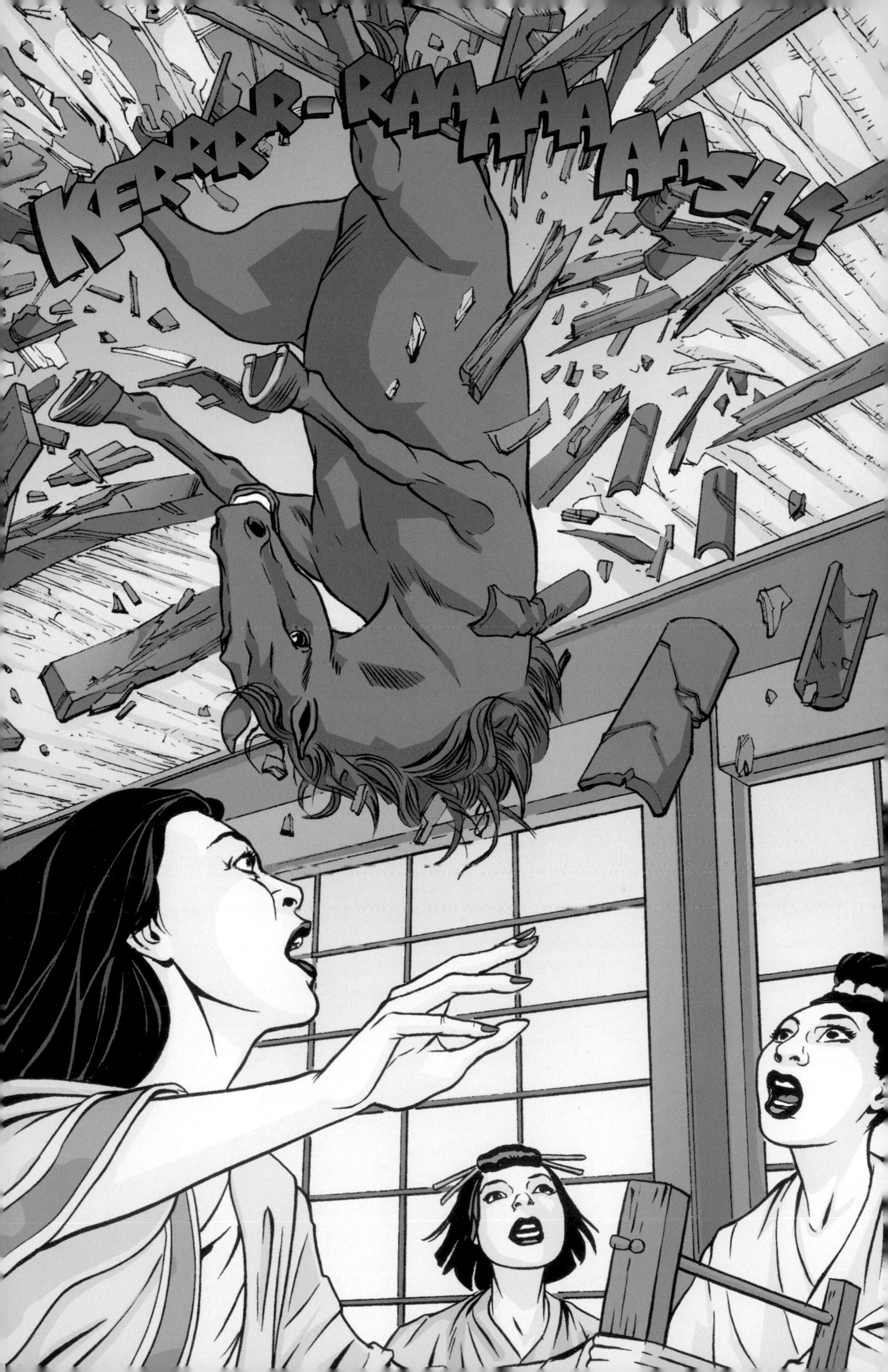
KERRRR-RAAAAAAAASH!

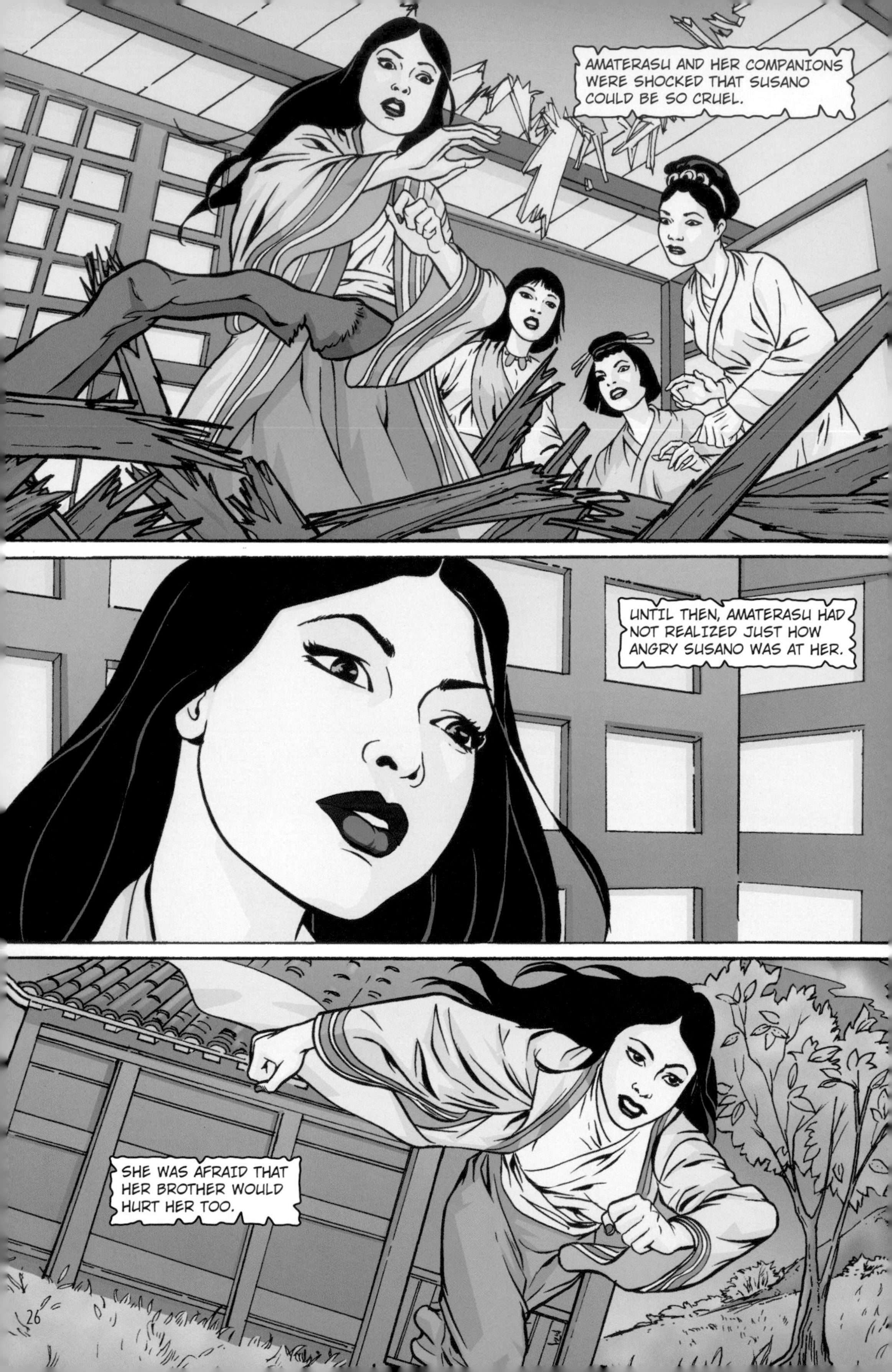
AMATERASU AND HER COMPANIONS WERE SHOCKED THAT SUSANO COULD BE SO CRUEL.
UNTIL THEN, AMATERASU HAD NOT REALIZED JUST HOW ANGRY SUSANO WAS AT HER.
SHE WAS AFRAID THAT HER BROTHER WOULD HURT HER TOO.

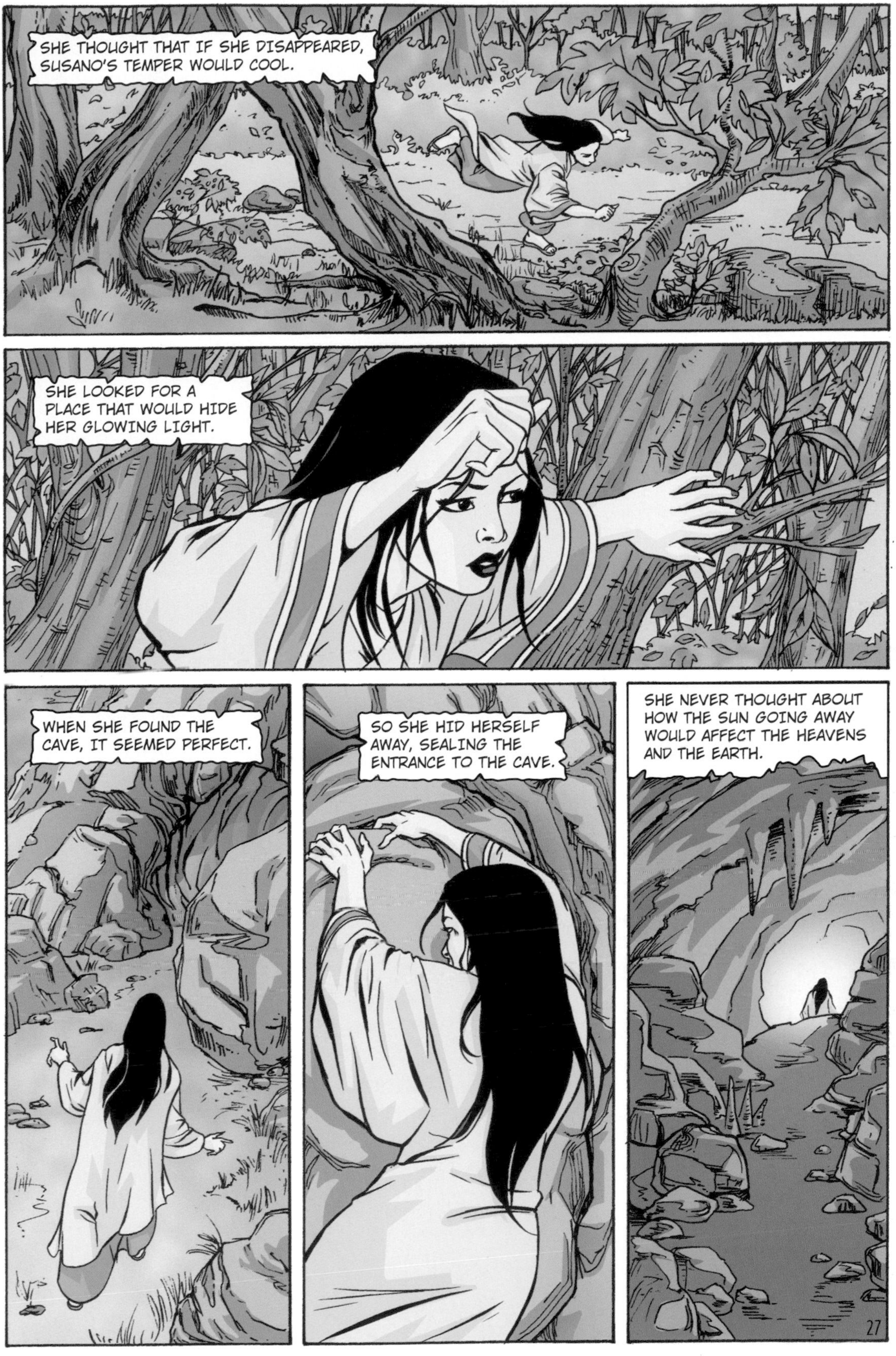
SHE THOUGHT THAT IF SHE DISAPPEARED, SUSANO'S TEMPER WOULD COOL.
SHE LOOKED FOR A PLACE THAT WOULD HIDE HER GLOWING LIGHT.
WHEN SHE FOUND THE CAVE, IT SEEMED PERFECT.
SO SHE HID HERSELF AWAY, SEALING THE ENTRANCE TO THE CAVE.
SHE NEVER THOUGHT ABOUT HOW THE SUN GOING AWAY WOULD AFFECT THE HEAVENS AND THE EARTH.

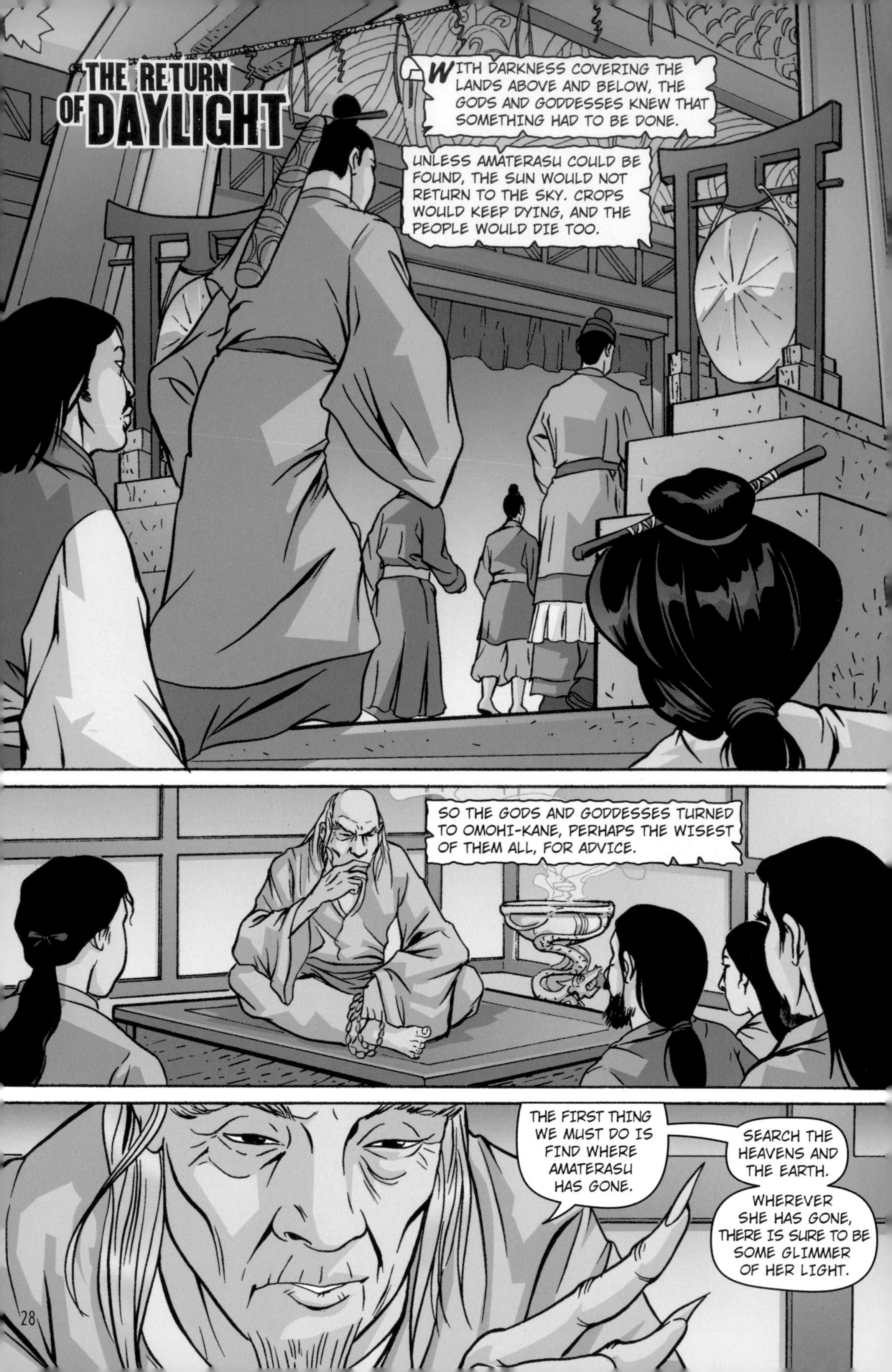
THE RETURN OF DAYLIGHT
WITH DARKNESS COVERING THE LANDS ABOVE AND BELOW, THE GODS AND GODDESSES KNEW THAT SOMETHING HAD TO BE DONE.
UNLESS AMATERASU COULD BE FOUND, THE SUN WOULD NOT RETURN TO THE SKY. CROPS WOULD KEEP DYING, AND THE PEOPLE WOULD DIE TOO.
SO THE GODS AND GODDESSES TURNED TO OMOHI-KANE, PERHAPS THE WISEST OF THEM ALL, FOR ADVICE.
THE FIRST THING WE MUST DO IS FIND WHERE AMATERASU HAS GONE.
SEARCH THE HEAVENS AND THE EARTH.
WHEREVER SHE HAS GONE, THERE IS SURE TO BE SOME GLIMMER OF HER LIGHT.

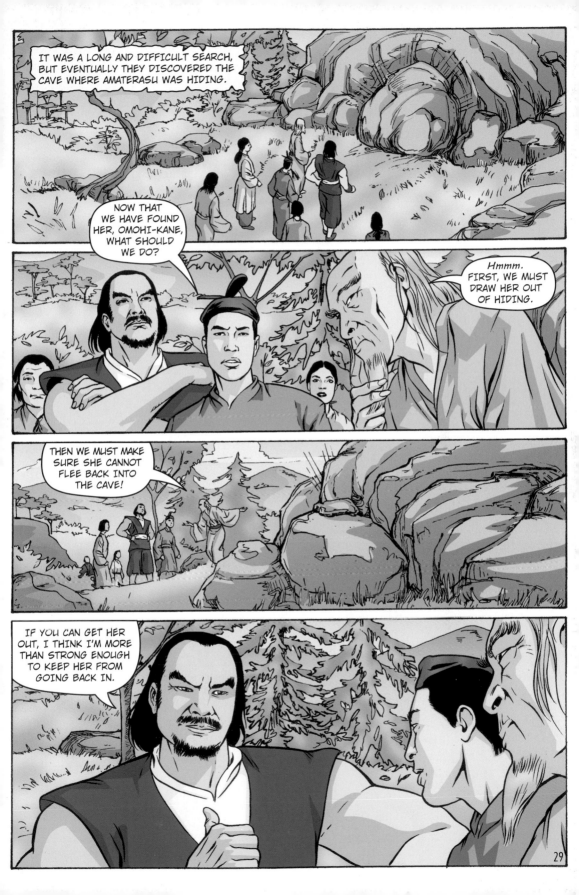

IT WAS A LONG AND DIFFICULT SEARCH, BUT EVENTUALLY THEY DISCOVERED THE CAVE WHERE AMATERASU WAS HIDING.

NOW THAT WE HAVE FOUND HER, OMOHI-KANE, WHAT SHOULD WE DO?

Hmmm. FIRST, WE MUST DRAW HER OUT OF HIDING.

THEN WE MUST MAKE SURE SHE CANNOT FLEE BACK INTO THE CAVE!

IF YOU CAN GET HER OUT, I THINK I'M MORE THAN STRONG ENOUGH TO KEEP HER FROM GOING BACK IN.

29

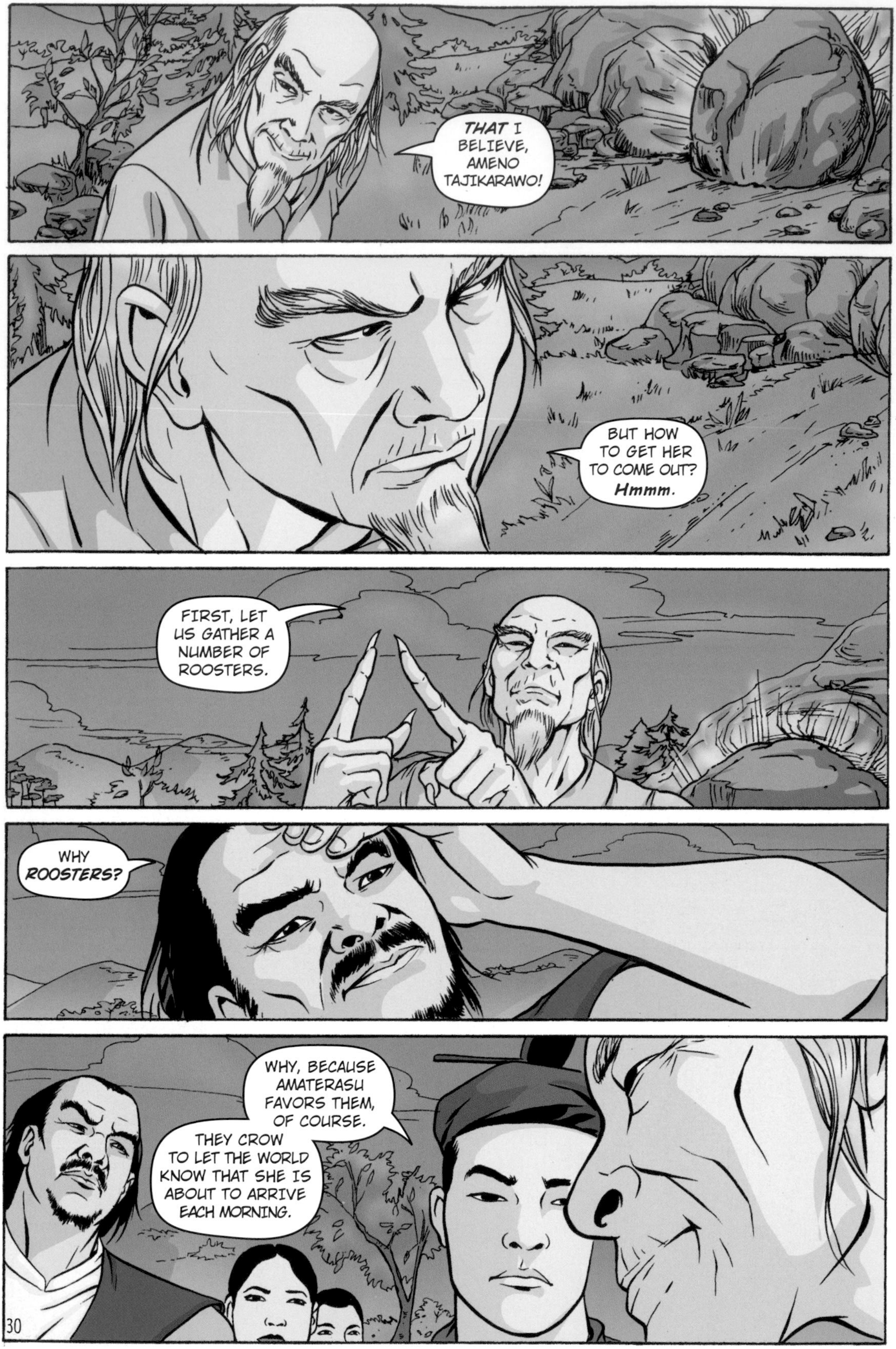
THAT I BELIEVE, AMENO TAJIKARAWO!
BUT HOW TO GET HER TO COME OUT? Hmmm.
FIRST, LET US GATHER A NUMBER OF ROOSTERS.
WHY ROOSTERS?
WHY, BECAUSE AMATERASU FAVORS THEM, OF COURSE.
THEY CROW TO LET THE WORLD KNOW THAT SHE IS ABOUT TO ARRIVE EACH MORNING.

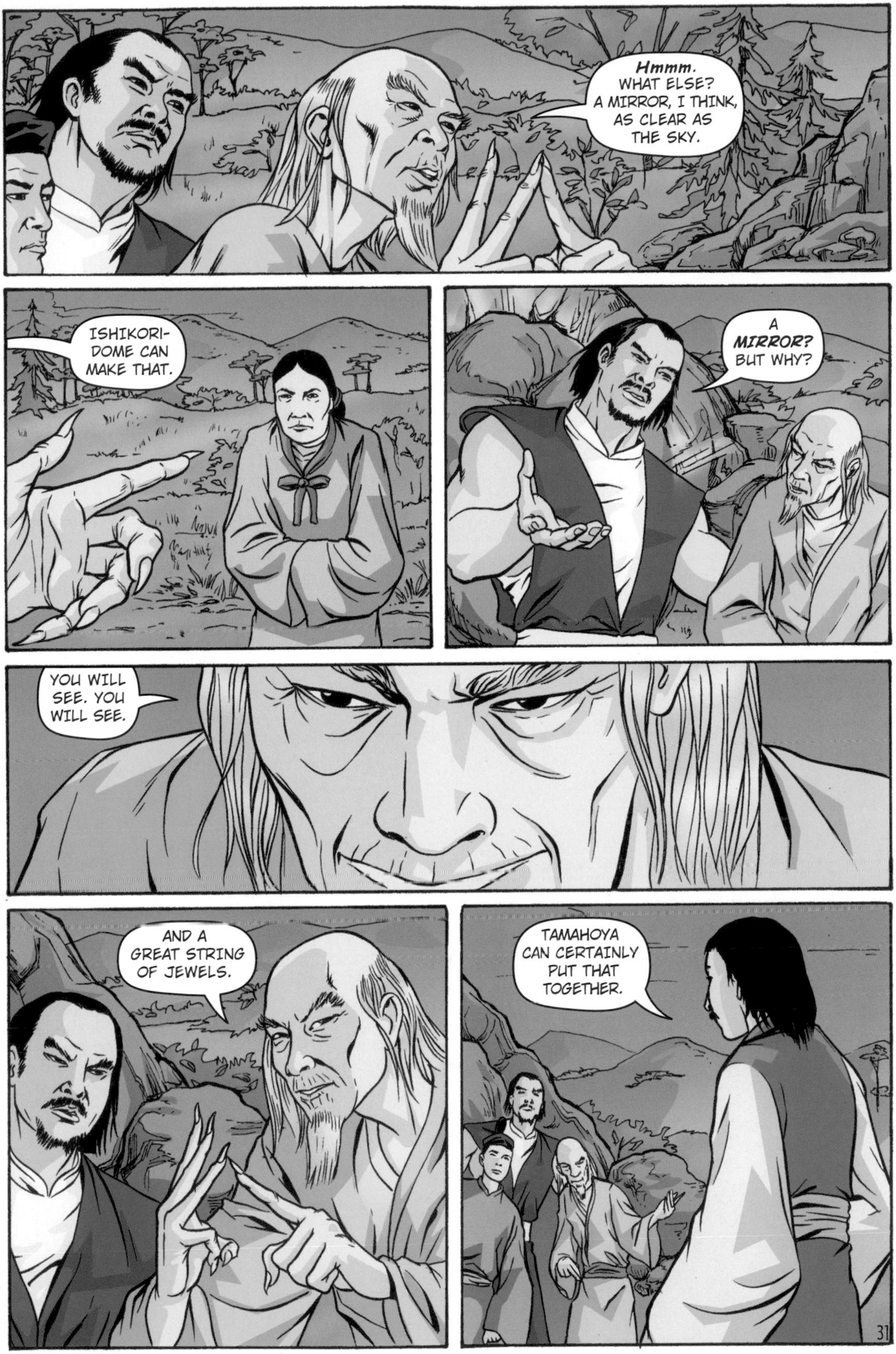
Hmmm. WHAT ELSE? A MIRROR, I THINK, AS CLEAR AS THE SKY.
ISHIKORI-DOME CAN MAKE THAT.
A *MIRROR?* BUT WHY?
YOU WILL SEE. YOU WILL SEE.
AND A GREAT STRING OF JEWELS.
TAMAHOYA CAN CERTAINLY PUT THAT TOGETHER.

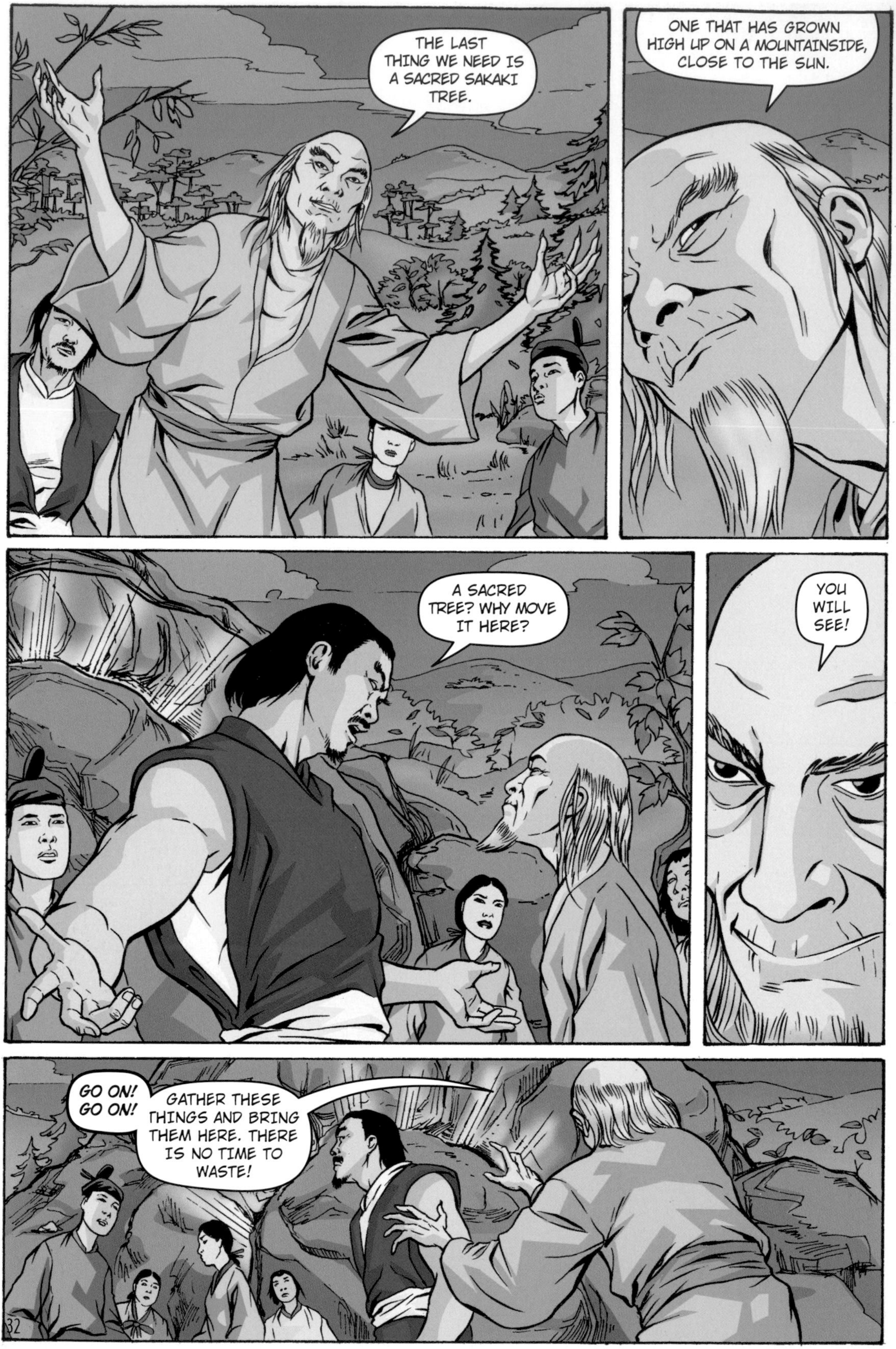
THE LAST THING WE NEED IS A SACRED SAKAKI TREE.
ONE THAT HAS GROWN HIGH UP ON A MOUNTAINSIDE, CLOSE TO THE SUN.
A SACRED TREE? WHY MOVE IT HERE?
YOU WILL SEE!
GO ON! GO ON!
GATHER THESE THINGS AND BRING THEM HERE. THERE IS NO TIME TO WASTE!

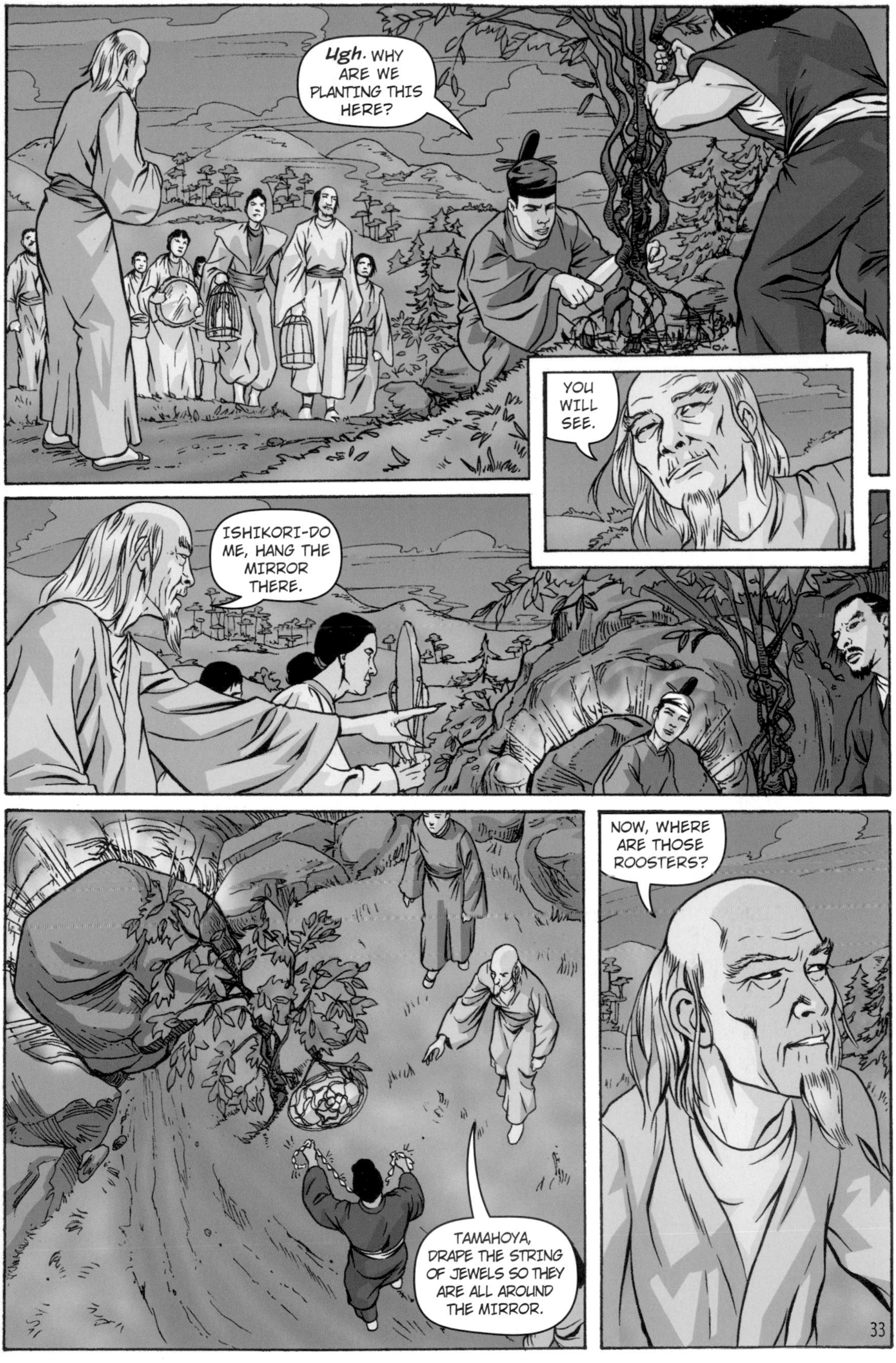
Ugh. WHY ARE WE PLANTING THIS HERE?
YOU WILL SEE.
ISHIKORI-DOME, HANG THE MIRROR THERE.
TAMAHOYA, DRAPE THE STRING OF JEWELS SO THEY ARE ALL AROUND THE MIRROR.
NOW, WHERE ARE THOSE ROOSTERS?

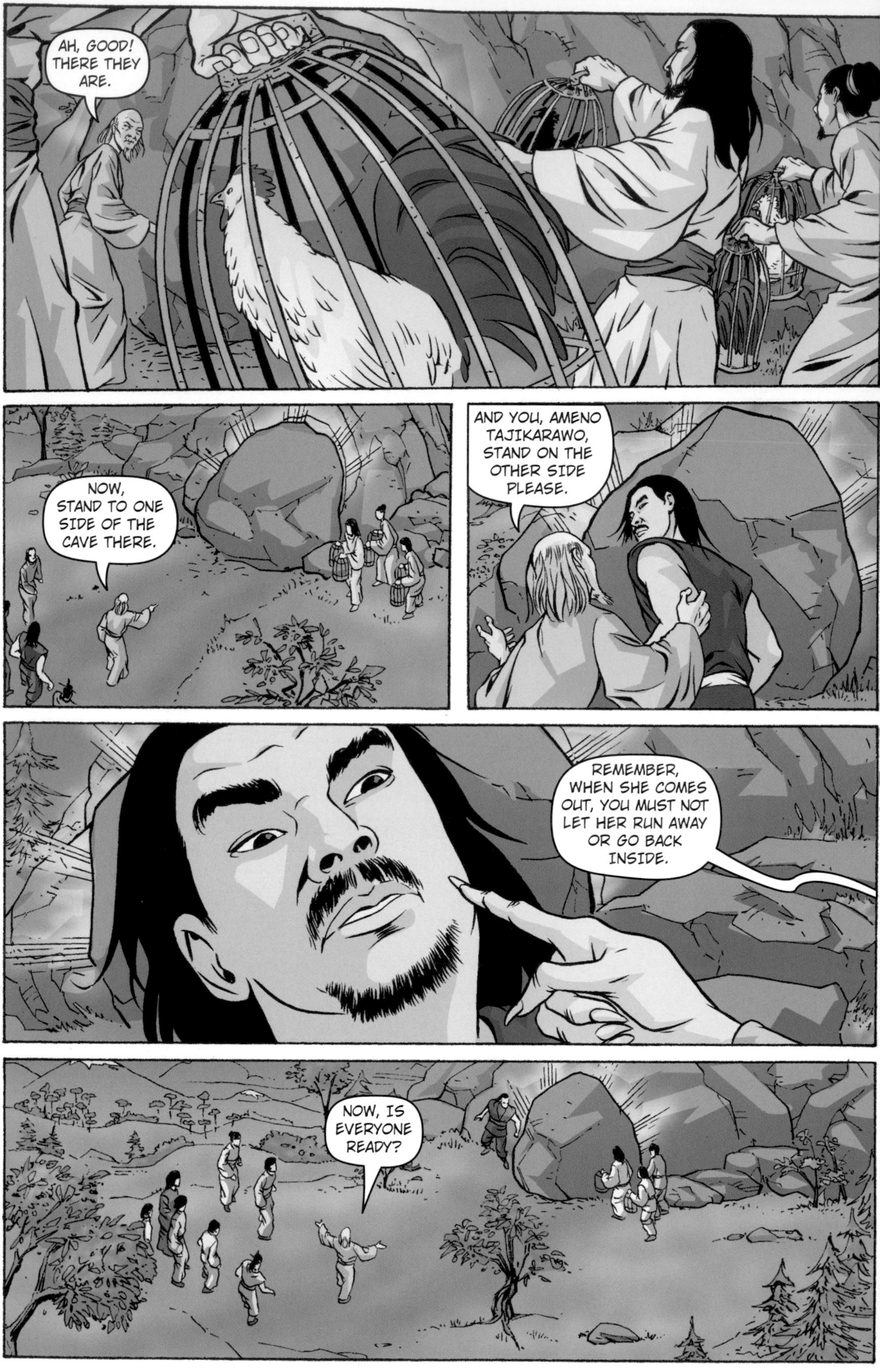
AH, GOOD! THERE THEY ARE.
NOW, STAND TO ONE SIDE OF THE CAVE THERE.
AND YOU, AMENO TAJIKARAWO, STAND ON THE OTHER SIDE PLEASE.
REMEMBER, WHEN SHE COMES OUT, YOU MUST NOT LET HER RUN AWAY OR GO BACK INSIDE.
NOW, IS EVERYONE READY?

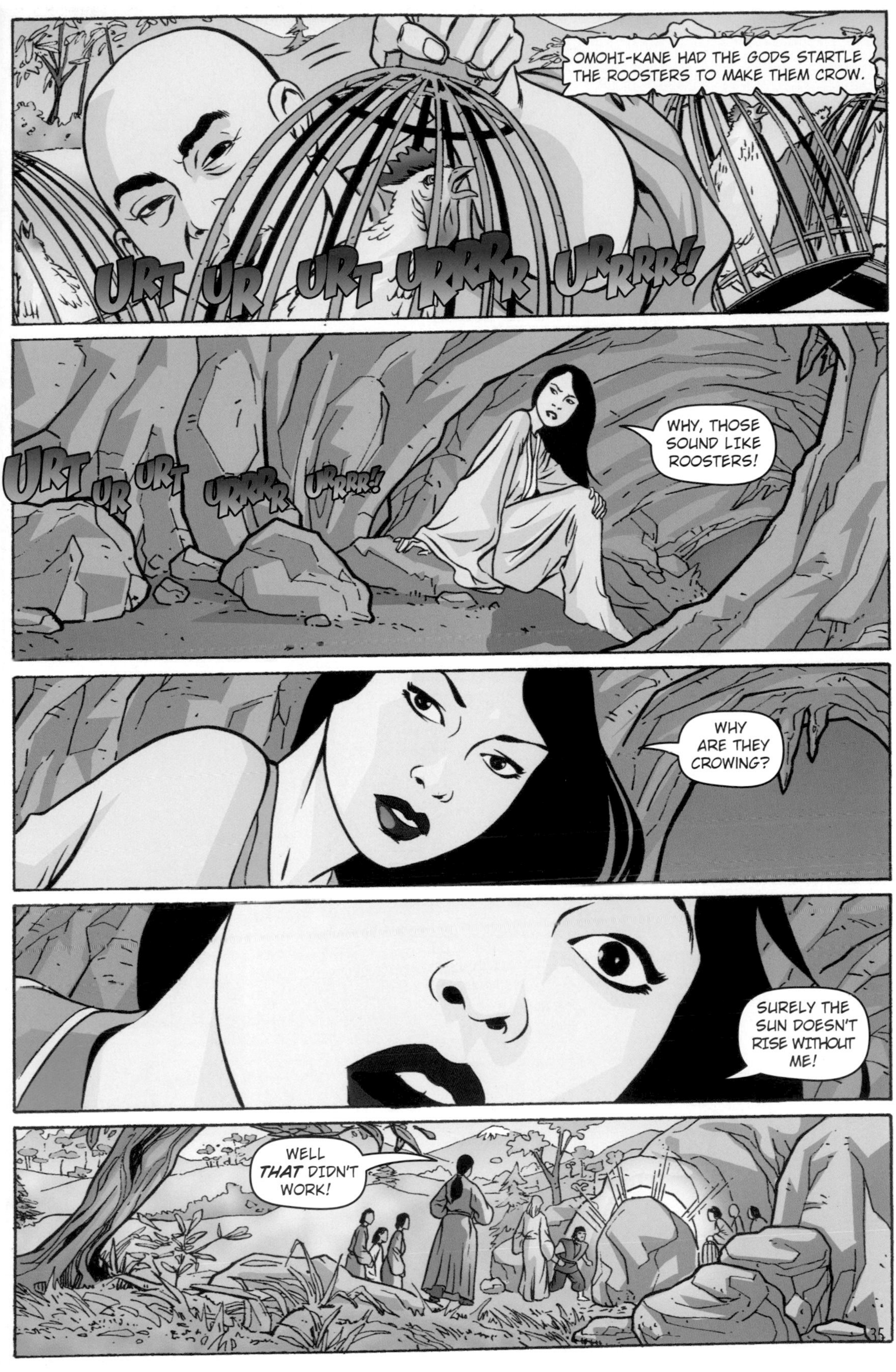
OMOHI-KANE HAD THE GODS STARTLE THE ROOSTERS TO MAKE THEM CROW.
URT UR URT URRRR URRRR!
URT UR URT URRRR URRRR!
WHY, THOSE SOUND LIKE ROOSTERS!
WHY ARE THEY CROWING?
SURELY THE SUN DOESN'T RISE WITHOUT ME!
WELL *THAT* DIDN'T WORK!

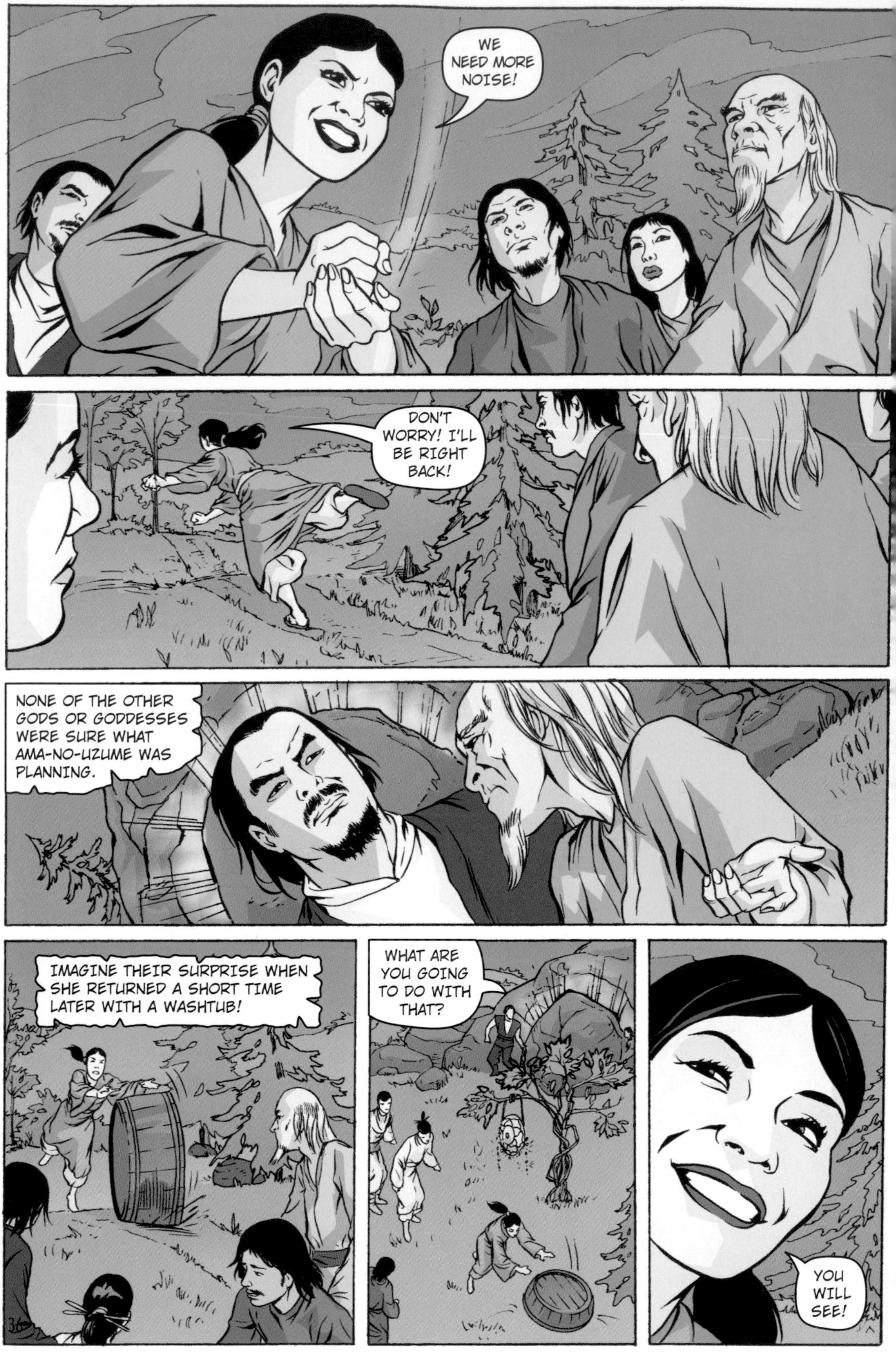
WE NEED MORE NOISE!
DON'T WORRY! I'LL BE RIGHT BACK!
NONE OF THE OTHER GODS OR GODDESSES WERE SURE WHAT AMA-NO-UZUME WAS PLANNING.
IMAGINE THEIR SURPRISE WHEN SHE RETURNED A SHORT TIME LATER WITH A WASHTUB!
WHAT ARE YOU GOING TO DO WITH THAT?
YOU WILL SEE!

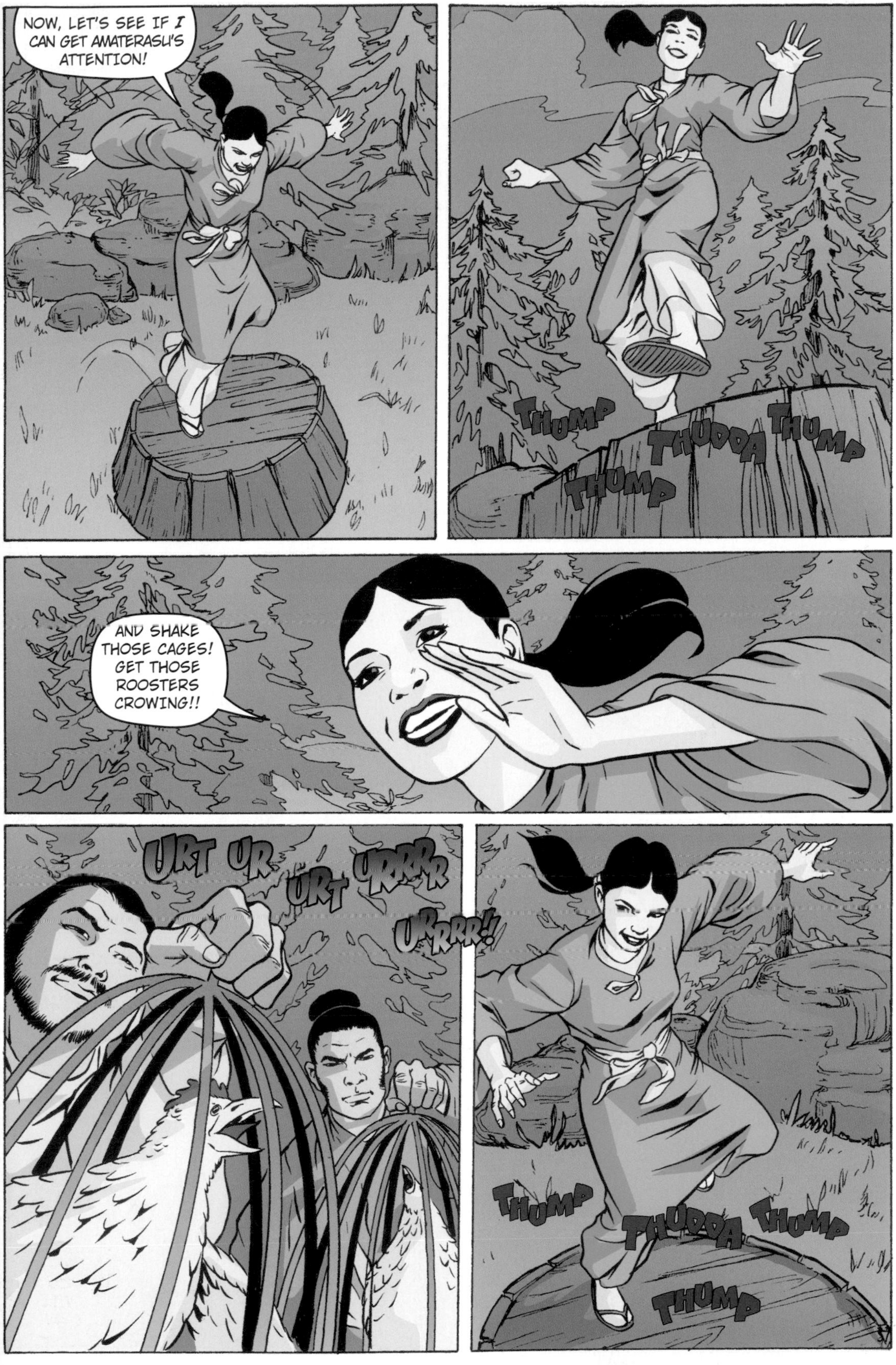
NOW, LET'S SEE IF I CAN GET AMATERASU'S ATTENTION!
THUMP
THUDDA
THUMP
THUMP
AND SHAKE THOSE CAGES! GET THOSE ROOSTERS CROWING!!
URT UR
URT
URRRR
URRRR!!
THUMP
THUDDA
THUMP
THUMP

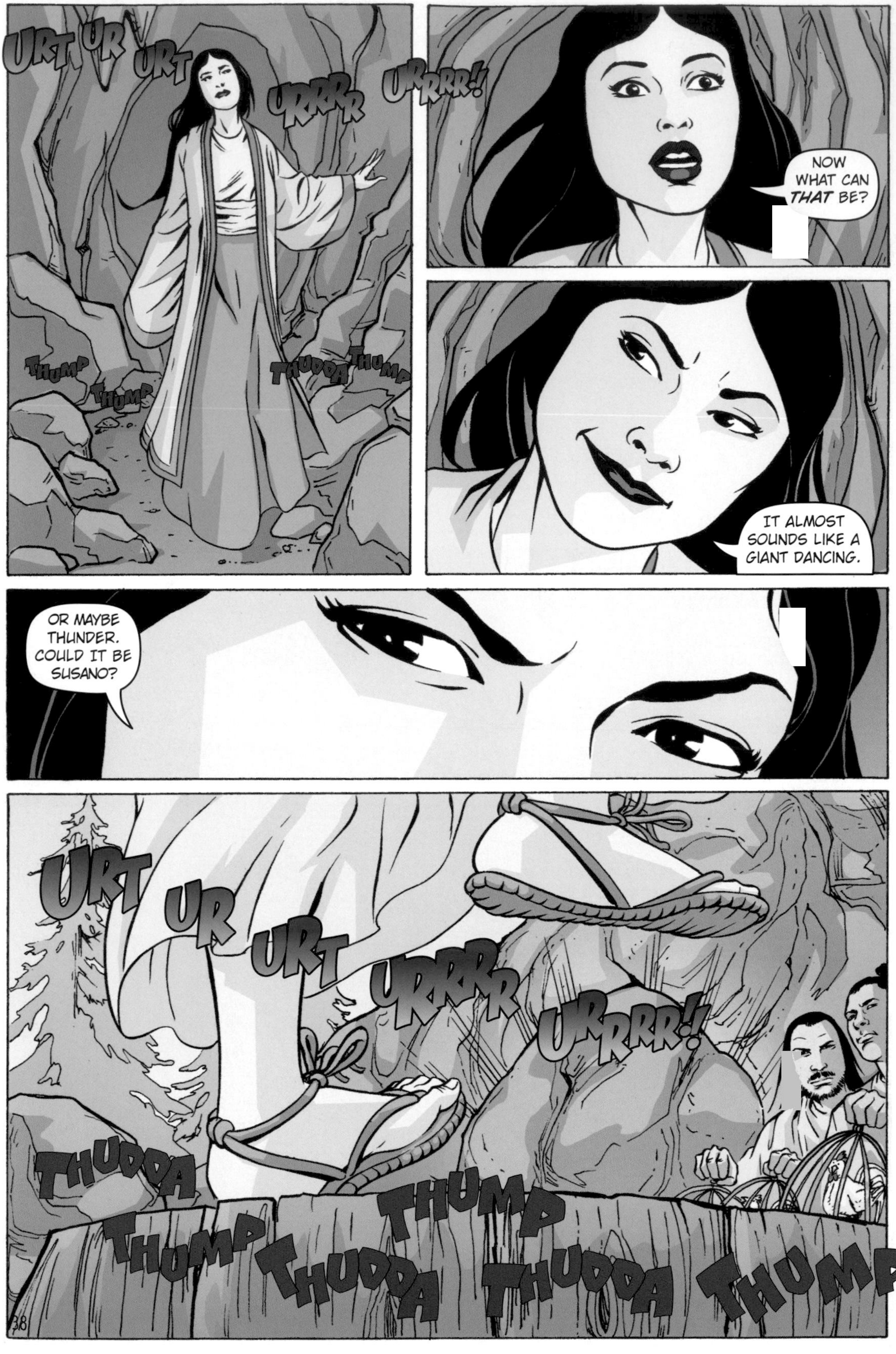
URT UR URT
URRRR URRRR!
THUMP THUMP
THUDDA THUMP
NOW WHAT CAN *THAT* BE?
IT ALMOST SOUNDS LIKE A GIANT DANCING.
OR MAYBE THUNDER. COULD IT BE SUSANO?
URT UR URT URRRR URRRR!
THUDDA
THUMP
THUMP
THUDDA
THUDDA
THUMP

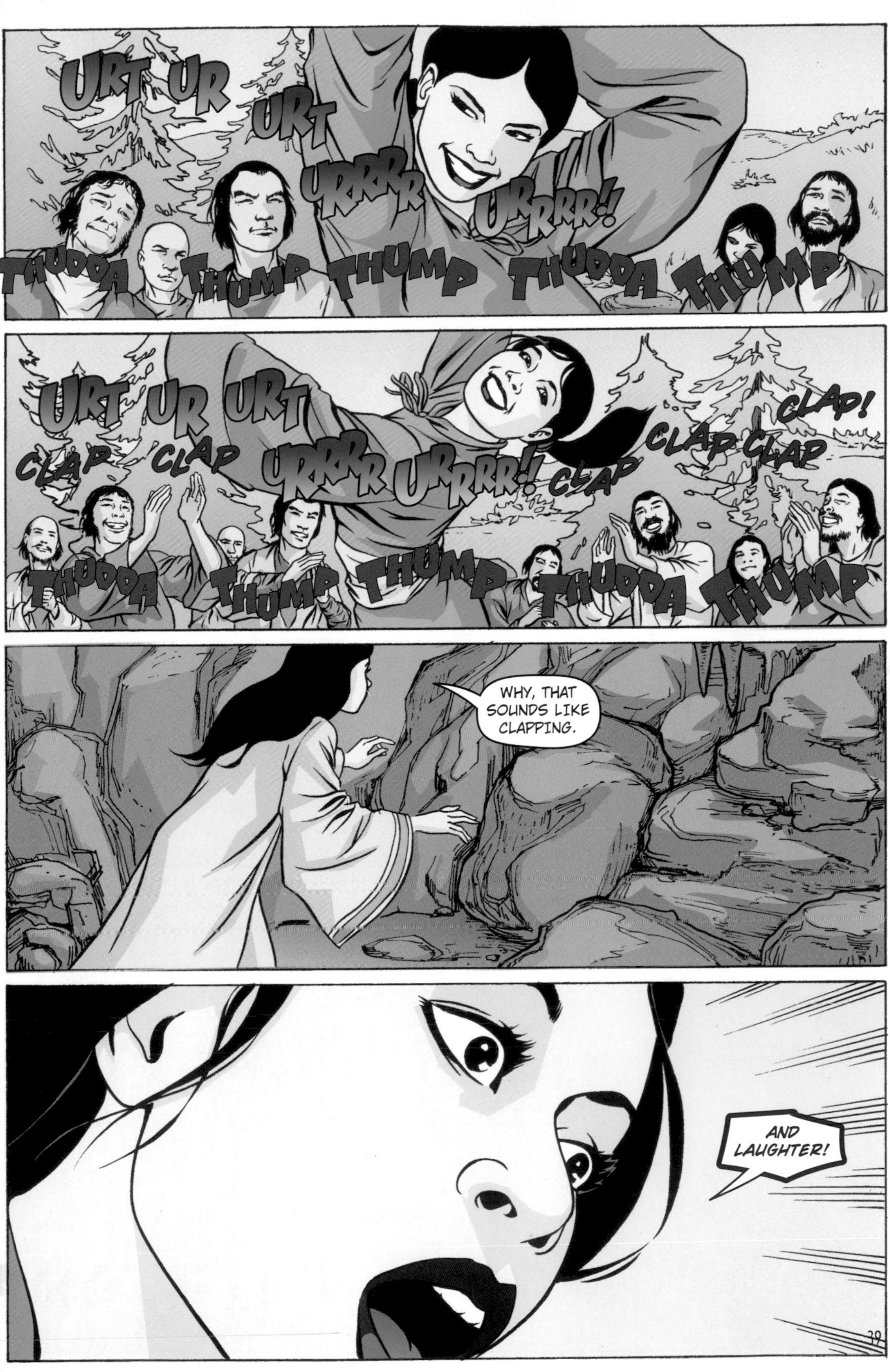
URT UR URT
URRRR URRRR!
THUDDA THUMP THUMP THUDDA THUMP
URT UR URT
CLAP CLAP
URRRR URRRR!
CLAP CLAP CLAP CLAP CLAP!
THUDDA THUMP THUMP THUDDA THUMP
WHY, THAT SOUNDS LIKE CLAPPING.
AND LAUGHTER!

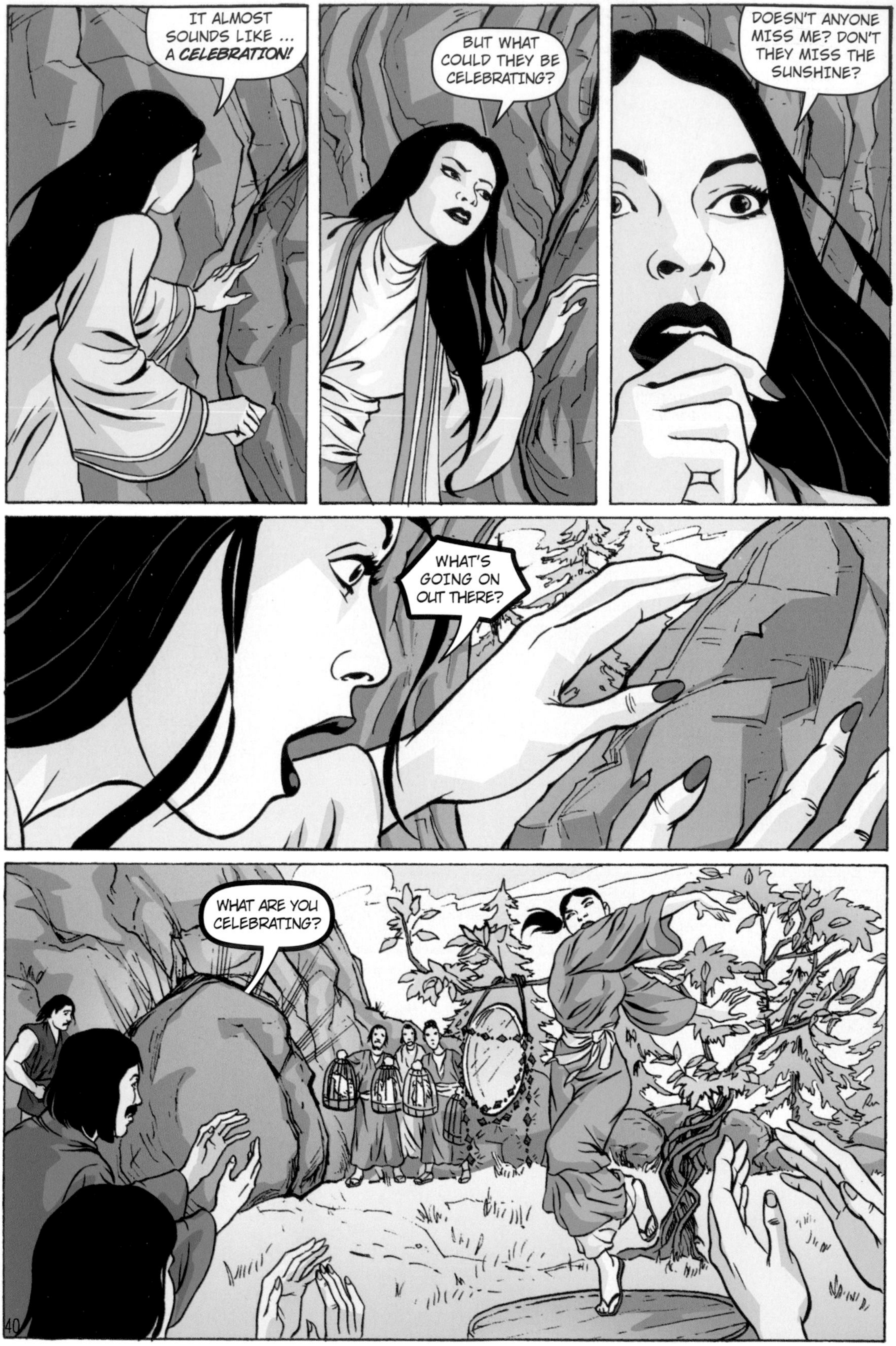
IT ALMOST SOUNDS LIKE ... A CELEBRATION!
BUT WHAT COULD THEY BE CELEBRATING?
DOESN'T ANYONE MISS ME? DON'T THEY MISS THE SUNSHINE?
WHAT'S GOING ON OUT THERE?
WHAT ARE YOU CELEBRATING?

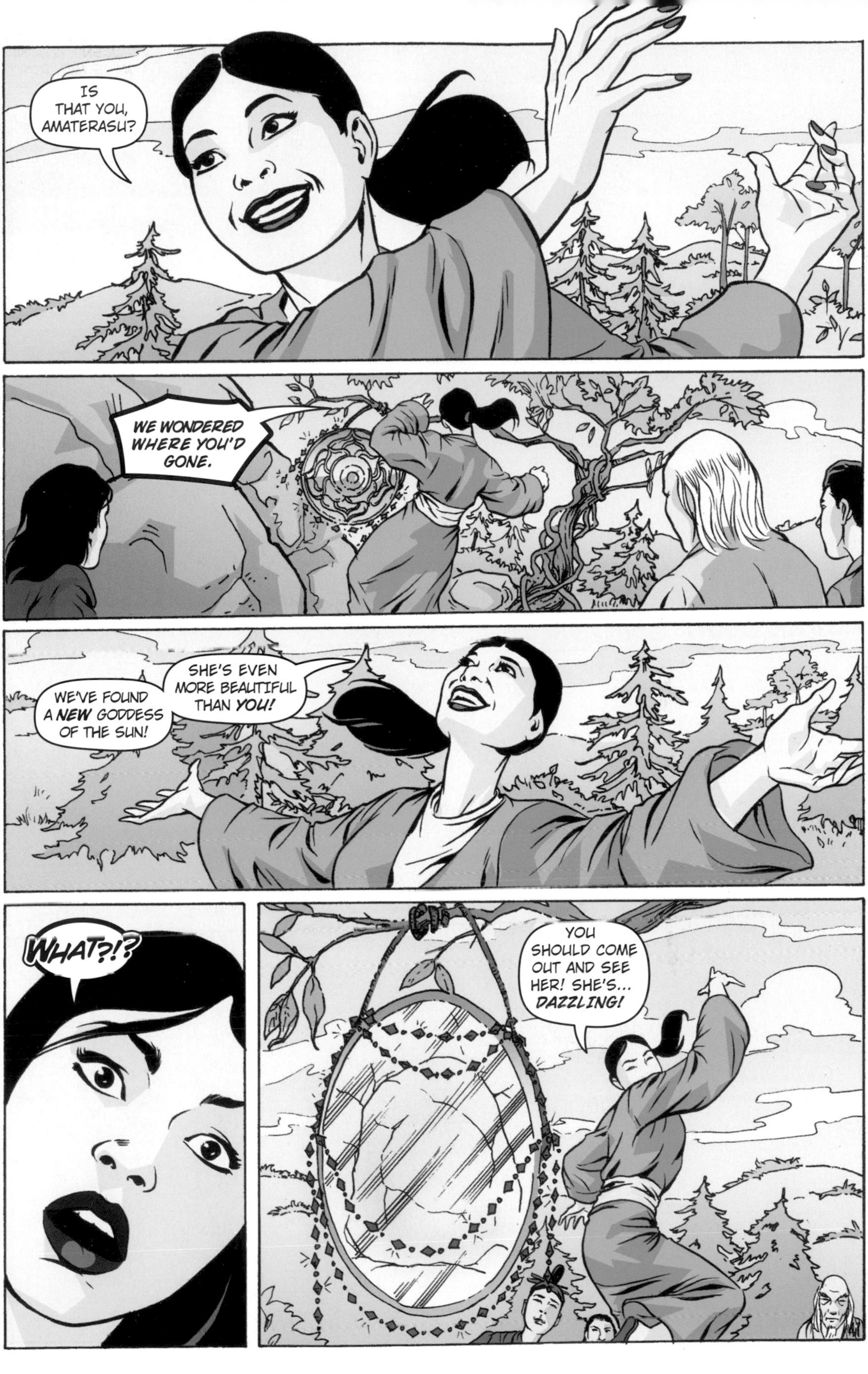
IS THAT YOU, AMATERASU?
WE WONDERED WHERE YOU'D GONE.
WE'VE FOUND A NEW GODDESS OF THE SUN!
SHE'S EVEN MORE BEAUTIFUL THAN YOU!
WHAT?!?
YOU SHOULD COME OUT AND SEE HER! SHE'S... DAZZLING!

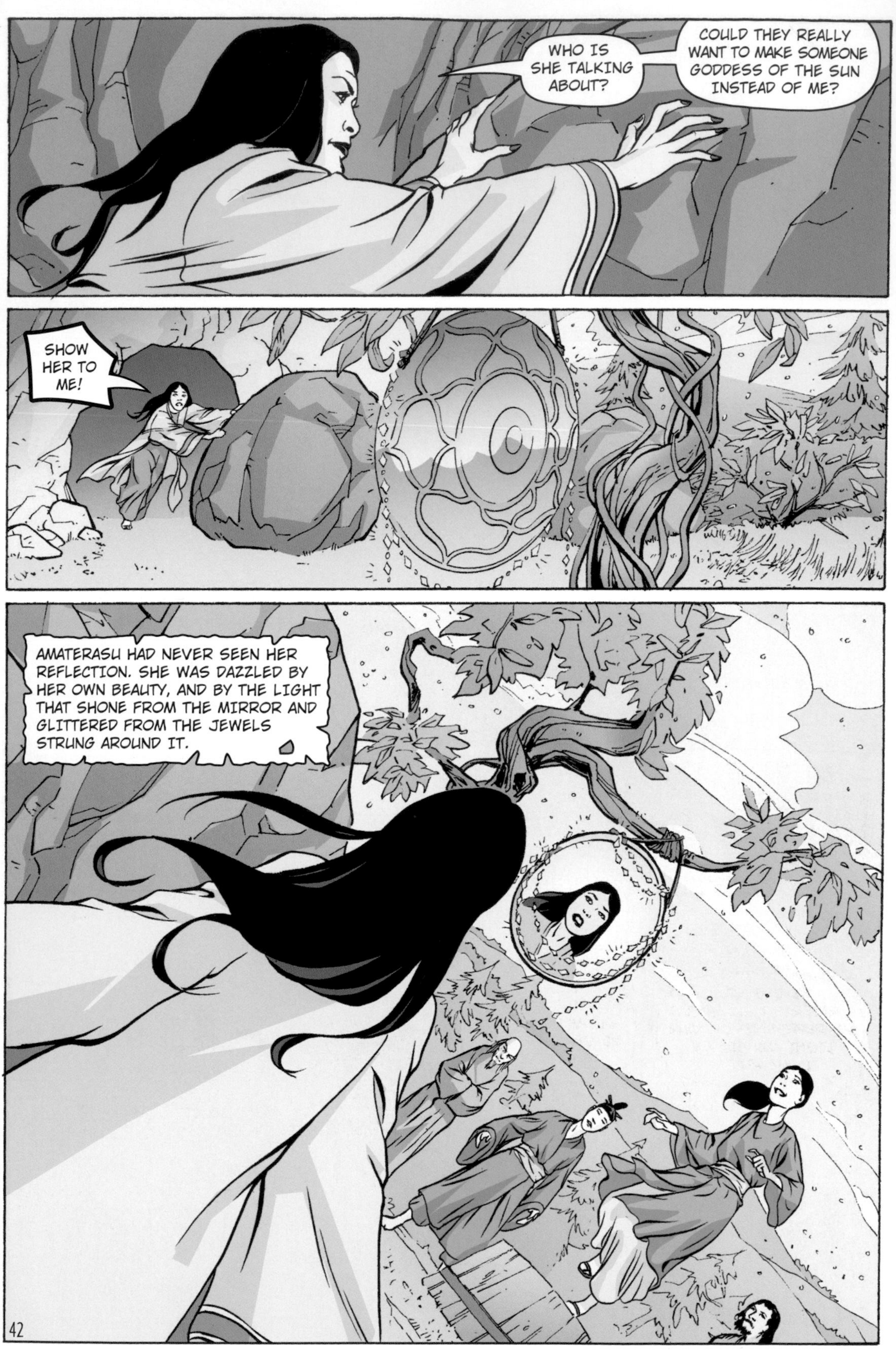
WHO IS SHE TALKING ABOUT?
COULD THEY REALLY WANT TO MAKE SOMEONE GODDESS OF THE SUN INSTEAD OF ME?
SHOW HER TO ME!
AMATERASU HAD NEVER SEEN HER REFLECTION. SHE WAS DAZZLED BY HER OWN BEAUTY, AND BY THE LIGHT THAT SHONE FROM THE MIRROR AND GLITTERED FROM THE JEWELS STRUNG AROUND IT.

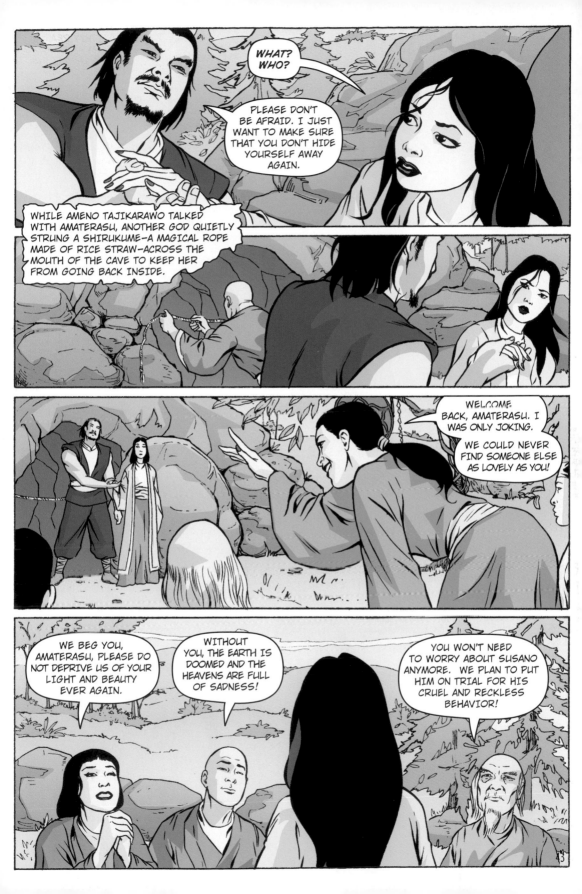

WHAT? WHO?

PLEASE DON'T BE AFRAID. I JUST WANT TO MAKE SURE THAT YOU DON'T HIDE YOURSELF AWAY AGAIN.

WHILE AMENO TAJIKARAWO TALKED WITH AMATERASU, ANOTHER GOD QUIETLY STRUNG A SHIRUKUME—A MAGICAL ROPE MADE OF RICE STRAW—ACROSS THE MOUTH OF THE CAVE TO KEEP HER FROM GOING BACK INSIDE.

WELCOME BACK, AMATERASU. I WAS ONLY JOKING.

WE COULD NEVER FIND SOMEONE ELSE AS LOVELY AS YOU!

WE BEG YOU, AMATERASU, PLEASE DO NOT DEPRIVE US OF YOUR LIGHT AND BEAUTY EVER AGAIN.

WITHOUT YOU, THE EARTH IS DOOMED AND THE HEAVENS ARE FULL OF SADNESS!

YOU WON'T NEED TO WORRY ABOUT SUSANO ANYMORE. WE PLAN TO PUT HIM ON TRIAL FOR HIS CRUEL AND RECKLESS BEHAVIOR!

43

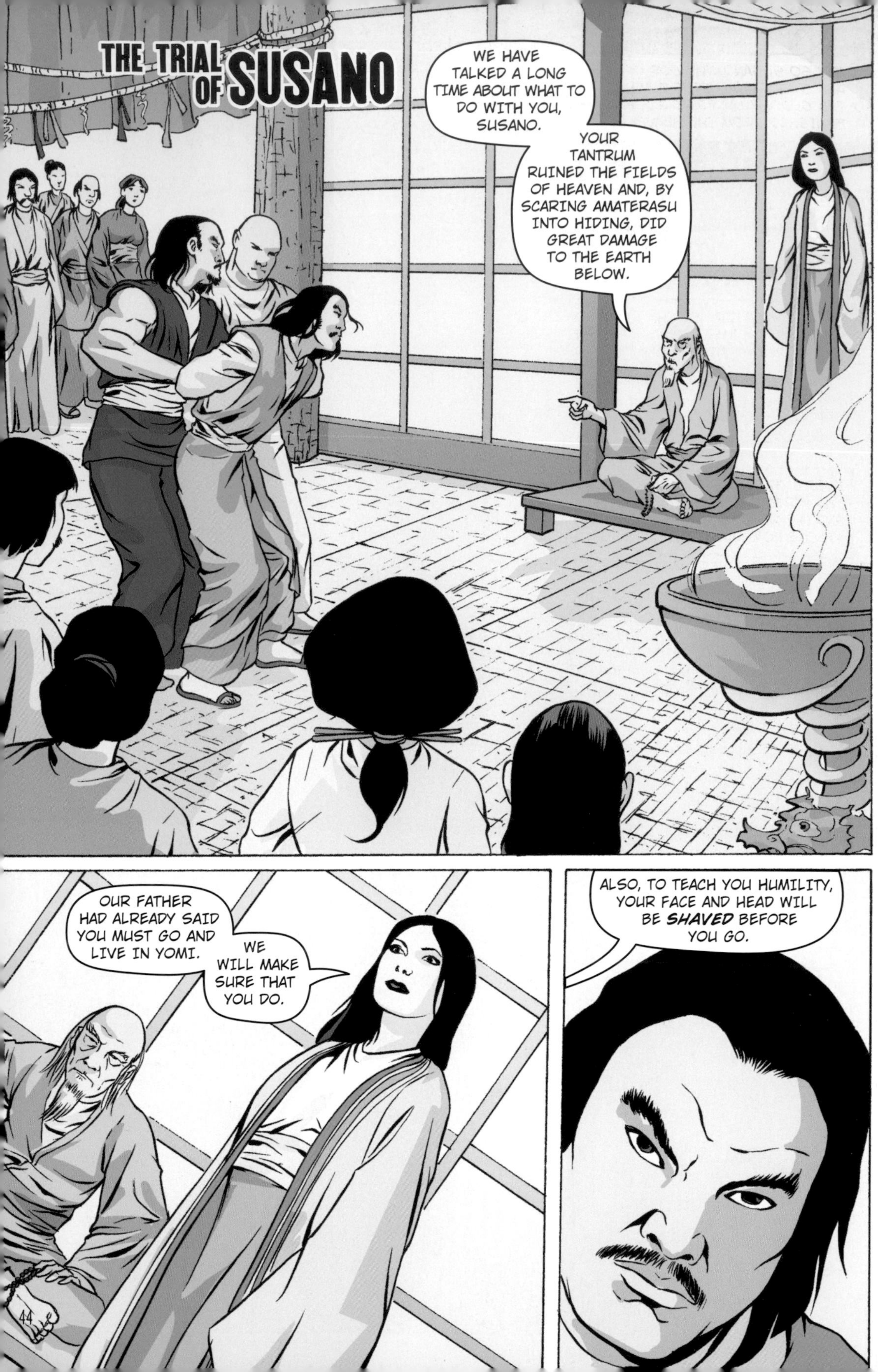
THE TRIAL OF SUSANO
WE HAVE TALKED A LONG TIME ABOUT WHAT TO DO WITH YOU, SUSANO.
YOUR TANTRUM RUINED THE FIELDS OF HEAVEN AND, BY SCARING AMATERASU INTO HIDING, DID GREAT DAMAGE TO THE EARTH BELOW.
OUR FATHER HAD ALREADY SAID YOU MUST GO AND LIVE IN YOMI.
WE WILL MAKE SURE THAT YOU DO.
ALSO, TO TEACH YOU HUMILITY, YOUR FACE AND HEAD WILL BE ***SHAVED*** BEFORE YOU GO.

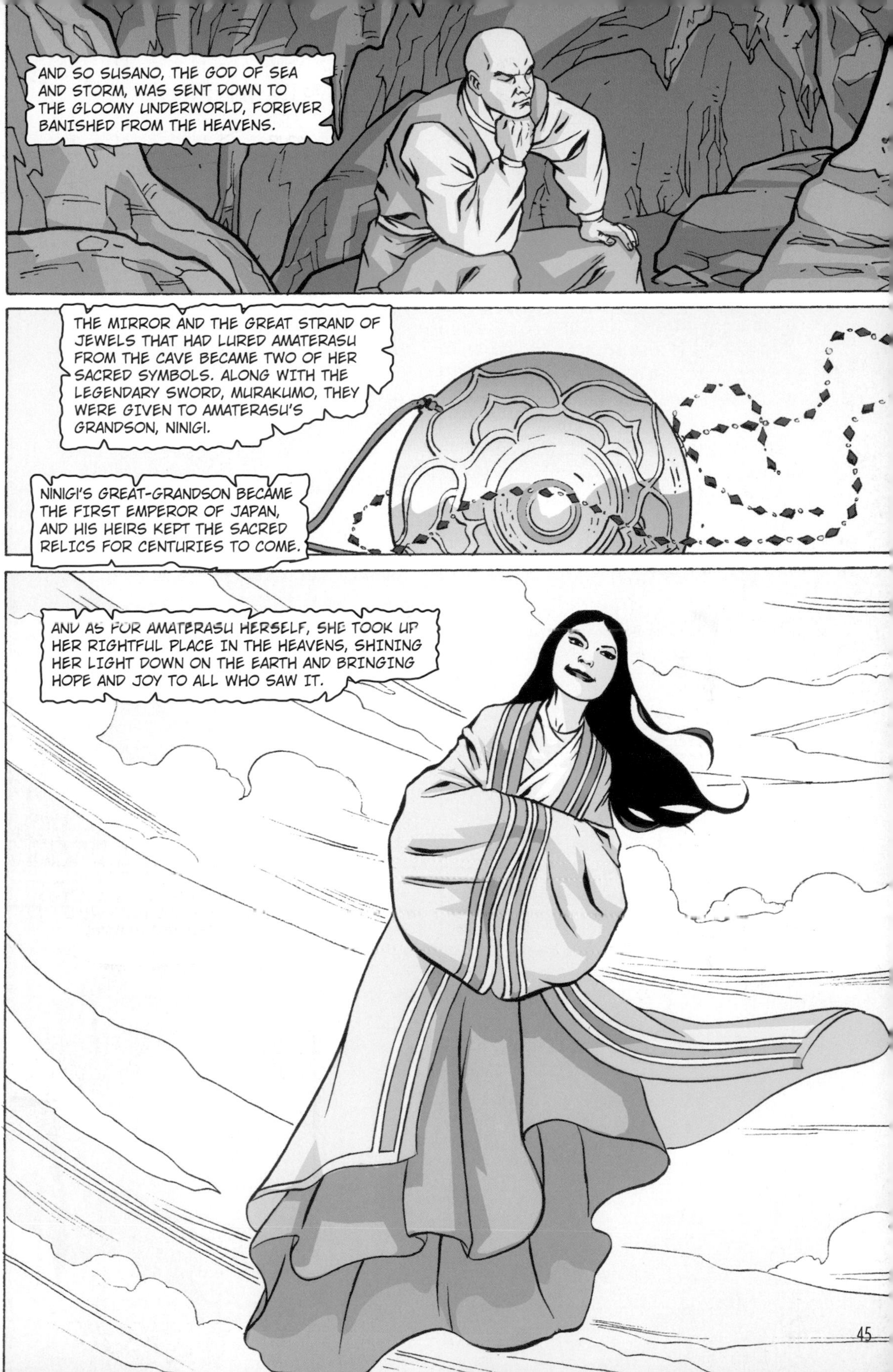
AND SO SUSANO, THE GOD OF SEA AND STORM, WAS SENT DOWN TO THE GLOOMY UNDERWORLD, FOREVER BANISHED FROM THE HEAVENS.
THE MIRROR AND THE GREAT STRAND OF JEWELS THAT HAD LURED AMATERASU FROM THE CAVE BECAME TWO OF HER SACRED SYMBOLS. ALONG WITH THE LEGENDARY SWORD, MURAKUMO, THEY WERE GIVEN TO AMATERASU'S GRANDSON, NINIGI.
NINIGI'S GREAT-GRANDSON BECAME THE FIRST EMPEROR OF JAPAN, AND HIS HEIRS KEPT THE SACRED RELICS FOR CENTURIES TO COME.
AND AS FOR AMATERASU HERSELF, SHE TOOK UP HER RIGHTFUL PLACE IN THE HEAVENS, SHINING HER LIGHT DOWN ON THE EARTH AND BRINGING HOPE AND JOY TO ALL WHO SAW IT.

GLOSSARY AND PRONUNCIATION GUIDE

AMA-NO-UZUME (*ah*-mah-no-oo-*zoo*-meh): the goddess of joy and happiness in the Japanese religion of Shinto

AMATERASU (*ah*-mah-teh-*rah*-soo): the Shinto goddess of the sun. Amaterasu is also revered as the inventor of wheat and rice cultivation, silk production, and loom weaving. In Japan, street processions and festivities in her honor are held each July 17. December 21 (the winter solstice) is also sacred. It marks the day she emerged from the cave and the sun returned.

AMENO TAJIKARAWO: (*ah*-meh-no tah-*jih*-kah-*rah*-woh): the Shinto god of strength

FIELDS OF HEAVEN: paradise, the home of the gods high above the earth

ISHIKORI-DOME (*ee*-shee-kor-ee *doo*-mee): a Shinto smith (someone who forges metal objects) goddess. She is credited with creating the mirror used to lure Amaterasu from her cave.

IZANAGI (ee-*zah*-nah-gee): the Shinto sky god who created the world with his wife, Izanami

IZANAMI (ee-*zah*-nah-mee): the Shinto earth goddess who created the world with her husband, Izanagi

KAMI (*kah*-mee): divine spirits. Kami can take the form of gods and goddesses, and they are also found throughout nature.

OMOHI-KANE (oh-*moh*-jih-*kah*-neh): a Shinto god of wisdom

SHIKOME (shih-*koh*-meh): foul women who inhabit Yomi

SHINTO: the native religion of Japan. *Shinto* means "the way of the gods." Shinto includes many gods and spirits, prayer and traditional ceremonies, and special foods.

SUSANO (soo-*sah*-noh): the Shinto god of the seas and of storms

TSUKIYOMI (too-*kee*-yoh-mee): the Shinto god of the moon

YOMI (*yoh*-mee): the land of the dead

original pencil sketch from page 27

46

FURTHER READING AND WEBSITES

Behnke, Alison. *Japan in Pictures*. Minneapolis: Twenty-First Century Books, 2003. This book features maps and full-color photographs illustrating Japanese geography, history, and culture.

Japanese-Myths.com.
   http://www.japanese-myths.com/index.htm. This site features information on Japan's gods and goddesses, heroes, and monsters.

Jingu.
   http://www.isejingu.or.jp/english/index.htm. This website explains Amaterasu's Shinto shrine, Ise Jingu. "Manga: Ise Jingu" is an illustrated section for kids on activities at the shrine, the tale of Amaterasu's mirror, and more stories about the goddess.

McAlpine, Helen, and William McAlpine. *Tales from Japan*. Oxford, UK: Oxford University Press, 2002. Originally published in 1958, the McAlpines' classic book retells Japanese myths and folktales.

"Religion and Ethics: Shinto." *BBC.co.uk.*
   http://www.bbc.co.uk/religion/religions/shinto/. The British Broadcasting Corporation's website looks at the basic beliefs and traditions of Shinto, the native religion of Japan.

Richardson, Hazel. *Life in Ancient Japan*. New York: Crabtree Publishing Company, 2005. Richardson details the events and cultural influences that shaped early Japan. Topics include the beginning of rice cultivation, the development of towns and trade, and the rise of religions, including Shinto.

CREATING *AMATERASU: RETURN OF THE SUN*

As with many myths and legends, some details about Amaterasu's tale vary. In creating this story, author Paul Storrie relied on *Realm of the Rising Sun: Japanese Myth* (edited by Tony Allan *et al.*), the *Encyclopedia of Eastern Myth*, and other sources on Asian mythology. Artist Ron Randall used details from Japanese art, costume museums, and traditional architecture to shape the story's visual details—from Amaterasu's gown to the mirror used to lure her out of the cave. Yuiko Kimura of the Minneapolis Institute of Arts used her knowledge of Japanese culture and art to ensure content and visual accuracy.

INDEX

ABOUT THE AUTHOR AND THE ARTIST

PAUL D. STORRIE was born and raised in Detroit, Michigan. He has returned to live there again and again after living in other cities and states. He began writing professionally in 1987 and has written comics for Caliber Comics, Moonstone Books, Marvel Comics, and DC Comics. Titles he has worked on include *Hercules, Robin Hood, Robyn of Sherwood* (featuring stories about Robin Hood's daughter), *Batman Beyond, Gotham Girls, Captain America: Red, White and Blue,* and *Mutant X.*

RON RANDALL has drawn comics for every major comic publisher in the United States, including Marvel, DC, Image, and Dark Horse. His work includes *Thor and Loki: In the Land of Giants, Justice League,* and *Spiderman.* He has created art for a wide range of genres, including science fiction (*Star Wars* and *Star Trek*), fantasy-adventure (*DragonLance* and *Warlord*), suspense and horror (*SwampThing, Predator,* and *Venom*), and his own title, *Trekker.* He lives in Portland, Oregon.